Drunk Driving

Other Books in the Social Issues Firsthand Series:

Drunk Driving

Stefan Kiesbye, Book Editor

GREENHAVEN PRESS
A part of Gale, Cengage Learning

GALE
CENGAGE Learning

Detroit • New York • San Francisco • New Haven, Conn • Waterville, Maine • London

HE
5620
.D72
D78
2008

Christine Nasso, *Publisher*
Elizabeth Des Chenes, *Managing Editor*

© 2008 Greenhaven Press, a part of Gale, Cengage Learning

For more information, contact:
Greenhaven Press
27500 Drake Rd.
Farmington Hills, MI 48331-3535
Or you can visit our Internet site at gale.cengage.com

For product information and technology assistance, contact us at

Gale Customer Support, 1-800-877-4253
For permission to use material from this text or product, submit all requests online at
www.cengage.com/permissions

Further permissions questions can be emailed to permissionrequest@cengage.com

Articles in Greenhaven Press anthologies are often edited for length to meet page requirements. In addition, original titles of these works are changed to clearly present the main thesis and to explicitly indicate the author's opinion. Every effort is made to ensure that Greenhaven Press accurately reflects the original intent of the authors. Every effort has been made to trace the owners of copyrighted material.

Cover photograph reproduced by permission of image copyright Igor Balasanov, 2008. Used under license from Shutterstock.com.

LIBRARY OF CONGRESS CATALOGING-IN-PUBLICATION DATA

Drunk driving / Stefan Kiesbye, book editor.
    p. cm. -- (Social issues firsthand)
Includes bibliographical references and index.
ISBN-13: 978-0-7377-4031-8 (hardcover)
1. Drunk driving--United States. 2. Drunk driving--United States--Prevention. I. Kiesbye, Stefan.
    HE5620.D72D78 2008
    363.12'57--dc22

2008014661

Printed in the United States of America
1 2 3 4 5 6 7 12 11 10 09 08

Contents

Chapter 1: The Toll of Drunk Driving

Chapter 2: Drunk Drivers Speak Out

Chapter 3: Taking Action Against Drunk Driving

Foreword

Social issues are often viewed in abstract terms. Pressing challenges such as poverty, homelessness, and addiction are viewed as problems to be defined and solved. Politicians, social scientists, and other experts engage in debates about the extent of the problems, their causes, and how best to remedy them. Often overlooked in these discussions is the human dimension of the issue. Behind every policy debate over poverty, homelessness, and substance abuse, for example, are real people struggling to make ends meet, to survive life on the streets, and to overcome addiction to drugs and alcohol. Their stories are ubiquitous and compelling. They are the stories of everyday people—perhaps your own family members or friends—and yet they rarely influence the debates taking place in state capitols, the national Congress, or the courts.

The disparity between the public debate and private experience of social issues is well illustrated by looking at the topic of poverty. Each year the U.S. Census Bureau establishes a poverty threshold. A household with an income below the threshold is defined as poor, while a household with an income above the threshold is considered able to live on a basic subsistence level. For example, in 2003 a family of two was considered poor if its income was less than $12,015; a family of four was defined as poor if its income was less than $18,810. Based on this system, the bureau estimates that 35.9 million Americans (12.5 percent of the population) lived below the poverty line in 2003, including 12.9 million children below the age of eighteen.

Commentators disagree about what these statistics mean. Social activists insist that the huge number of officially poor Americans translates into human suffering. Even many families that have incomes above the threshold, they maintain, are likely to be struggling to get by. Other commentators insist that the statistics exaggerate the problem of poverty in the United States. Compared to people in developing countries, they point out, most so-called poor families have a high quality of life. As stated by journalist Fidelis Iyebote, "Cars are owned by 70 percent of 'poor' households. . . . Color televisions belong to 97 percent of the 'poor' [and] videocassette recorders belong to nearly 75 percent. . . . Sixty-four percent have microwave ovens, half own a stereo system, and over a quarter possess an automatic dishwasher."

However, this debate over the poverty threshold and what it means is likely irrelevant to a person living in poverty. Simply put, poor people do not need the government to tell them whether they are poor. They can see it in the stack of bills they cannot pay. They are aware of it when they are forced to choose between paying rent or buying food for their children. They become painfully conscious of it when they lose their homes and are forced to live in their cars or on the streets. Indeed, the written stories of poor people define the meaning of poverty more vividly than a government bureaucracy could ever hope to. Narratives composed by the poor describe losing jobs due to injury or mental illness, depict horrific tales of childhood abuse and spousal violence, recount the loss of friends and family members. They evoke the slipping away of social supports and government assistance, the descent into substance abuse and addiction, the harsh realities of life on the streets. These are the perspectives on poverty that are too often omitted from discussions over the extent of the problem and how to solve it.

Greenhaven Press's Social Issues Firsthand series provides a forum for the often-overlooked human perspectives on society's most divisive topics of debate. Each volume focuses on one social issue and presents a collection of ten to sixteen narratives by those who have had personal involvement with the topic. Extra care has been taken to include a diverse range of perspectives. For example, in the volume on adoption, readers will find the stories of birth parents who have made an adoption plan, adoptive parents, and adoptees themselves. After exposure to these varied points of view, the reader will have a clearer understanding that adoption is an intense, emotional experience full of joyous highs and painful lows for all concerned.

The debate surrounding embryonic stem cell research illustrates the moral and ethical pressure that the public brings to bear on the scientific community. However, while nonexperts often criticize scientists for not considering the potential negative impact of their work, ironically the public's reaction against such discoveries can produce harmful results as well. For example, although the outcry against embryonic stem cell research in the United States has resulted in fewer embryos being destroyed, those with Parkinson's, such as actor Michael J. Fox, have argued that prohibiting the development of new stem cell lines ultimately will prevent a timely cure for the disease that is killing Fox and thousands of others.

Each book in the series contains several features that enhance its usefulness, including an in-depth introduction, an annotated table of contents, bibliographies for further research, a list of organizations to contact, and a thorough index. These elements—combined with the poignant voices of people touched by tragedy and triumph—make the Social Issues Firsthand series a valuable resource for research on today's topics of political discussion.

Introduction

A dinner with friends, a birthday celebration at a restaurant, a tailgate party, drinks at a bar after work. The car is parked nearby and it's only three miles to home. Of course nobody gets behind the wheel imagining the worst. Many adults have faced the dilemma—leave the car behind and call a cab or drive intoxicated as carefully as possible? Many take the risk and drive against their own better judgment.

In 2005, as the Centers for Disease Control and Prevention (CDC) reports, "16,885 people in the United States died in alcohol-related motor vehicle crashes, representing 39% of all traffic-related deaths. . . . Nearly 1.4 million drivers were arrested for driving under the influence of alcohol or narcotics. . . . That's less than 1% of the 159 million self-reported episodes of alcohol-impaired driving among U.S. adults each year."

On February 20, 1998, Daryl Dupuis was waiting at home for his fiancée Gina to come home from work. She had called earlier to ask him what he would like her to pick up for dinner. It was only a ten-minute drive, and Daryl was getting nervous as he waited for Gina's return. Then he saw the news on television. A crash on the nearby interstate had left two women seriously injured. Daryl drove to the scene to find out what had happened.

A female receptionist for a law firm had had several drinks at a local bar with her colleagues before deciding to drive home in her minivan. She entered the interstate via an off-ramp and continued to drive the wrong way for about two miles. Cars swerved to avoid her, but Daryl's fiancée noticed her too late to move out of the way. The two cars collided.

On his Web site, Daryl writes that Gina

> suffered severe head trauma. . . . Her reasoning, reading comprehension, information sorting, information process-

ing, and social skills were reduced. Gina had her lip tear up from [her] face on the right side of [her] mouth from contact with the dash resulting in a scar that will never go away. . . . She broke her left collarbone from the seat belt cross strap and her right side pelvis fractured into 3 parts. . . . Her sciatic nerve was damaged because the razor sharp broken bones cut into her nerve and this ended up causing Gina to have a dropped right foot, which she will have forever. She cannot lift her right foot or move her toes. . . . Severe arthritis is already set in and Gina had a hip replacement surgery done in 2003. She will need one every 25 years thereafter.

Daryl and Gina were married that same year, and the accident will forever be with them. The drunk driver ended up serving four years in prison, leaving her teenage children without a mother. The damage suffered as a result of the car crash went far beyond the physical injuries for all families involved.

Yet prison sentences, according to Professor David Hanson at the State University of New York, Potsdam, are of little use in solving the problem of drunk driving fatalities. "Jail or prison sentences for alcohol offenses, in spite of their great popularity, appear to be of little value in deterring high BAC [blood alcohol concentration] drivers. In short, it appears that we can't 'jail our way out of the problem.'" He claims that the "perception of swift and certain punishment is more important than severity."

Rather than simply putting offenders behind bars, Hanson advocates for driving while intoxicated (DWI) or driving under the influence (DUI) courts, sobriety courts, wellness courts, or accountability courts. He argues that they have been effective in cutting down on drunk driving incidents. "Such courts address the problem of hard-core repeat offenders by treating alcohol addiction or alcoholism. The recidivism or failure rate of DWI courts is very low," says Hanson.

Among the measures that could be taken to deter repeat offenders are: automatic license revocation along with a mandatory jail sentence; impounding or confiscating license plates; mandating the installation of interlock devices that prevent intoxicated persons from starting a vehicle; vehicle impoundment or immobilization; and educational programs to correct the mistaken perception that it's acceptable to occasionally drive under the influence of alcohol.

Mothers Against Drunk Driving (MADD) and other groups have had a major impact on educating people about the dangers of driving while intoxicated, thereby increasing the safety of America's roads. According to the National Highway Safety Administration (NHTSA), "There are now fewer than one and a half [overall] deaths (including the deaths of bicyclists, motorcyclists, pedestrians, auto drivers, and auto passengers) per one hundred million vehicle miles traveled." Alcohol-related traffic fatalities in particular also have dropped by over 20 percent in the past twenty-five years. Alcohol-related traffic deaths have dropped from 1.64 per 100 million miles traveled in 1982 down to 0.56 in 2005.

Anti-drunk-driving advocates urge drivers to act responsibly by not driving after drinking, arranging beforehand to have a ride available, and encouraging friends and family to do the same. As Hanson writes, "Volunteer to be a designated driver," and "don't ever let your friends drive drunk. Take their keys, have them stay the night, have them ride home with someone else, call a cab, or do whatever else is necessary—but don't let them drive!" The authors of *Social Issues Firsthand: Drunk Driving* explore the impact drunk driving has on accident victims and their friends and family, and offer solutions to decrease drunk driving accidents and fatalities.

CHAPTER 1

The Toll of
Drunk Driving

My Son Was Killed by a Drunk Driver

Bob Ledbetter

Through the sudden and violent death of his son Aaron and two other teenagers, the author not only experiences intense grief, but is also made painfully aware of the inadequate measures taken to prevent drunk driving. He does find some peace by donating his son's organs, however, and by befriending the recipients.

On February 18, 1995, in the small northwest Texas town of Bowie, a crash caused the deaths of three teenagers. Two died that night; my son Aaron, who was driving the car, died from his injuries eight days later.

The state reconstructive team determined that Aaron had done everything possible to avoid the crash. The other driver crossed all the way over the center line in his one-ton pickup loaded with oil equipment, and hit the teens head-on. Despite the testimony of witnesses as to his impairment, including law enforcement and other emergency responders, as well as a pickup full of beer cans, the driver refused to be tested for alcohol and was not forced to do so. Eventually the driver pled guilty to three counts of reckless manslaughter and was sentenced to 20 years. He'll get out after only eight years.

Death Was Not the End of the Tragedy

The two teens in the car with my son, Ruby and Chanse, died at the scene of the crash. Aaron was care-flighted [transported by emergency helicopter] to the hospital where my wife Margie and I were told that his injuries were so numerous and severe that he could die at any time. When we were given the news I said, "If he does die, I want you to take whatever organs you can use."

Organ donation wasn't something Aaron and I had ever talked about, but we are a family that helps others and I felt it was something he would have wanted.

Aaron was in surgery for seven and a half hours. He had multiple fractures in his left leg and his hip was dislocated. The spleen was damaged and was removed. His left elbow was crushed, his collarbone broken and there was extensive internal bleeding. The plastic surgeon said Aaron's face resembled a china plate that had been dropped onto a concrete floor. His left eye was dislodged from the socket, and he would probably be blind in that eye. But the most serious damage was the head trauma—two lobes of Aaron's brain had been torn apart. Eight days after the crash, Aaron was pronounced dead. He never regained consciousness.

The Pain Remains

We didn't know it at the time but our pain had just begun. We didn't understand that we had been sentenced to a lifetime of pain and sorrow. They say the pain gets easier; I think you just learn to live with it.

A representative from the organ procurement agency came to talk with us. The whole family was there as well as many close friends. There was no hesitation, we had all been searching for some ray of goodness to come from this tragedy and to be able to donate some of Aaron's organs seemed like one of those ways. Aaron had a compassion and tenderness unusual for a 17-year-old and we knew that somewhere there were people who needed his help.

The representative explained all the procedures in detail and answered our questions. We chose not to donate skin and tissue but wanted Aaron's kidneys and heart—the only organs not damaged—to help others. His corneas couldn't be transplanted but they could go to research so we agreed to that as well.

Organs Helped Other People Live

We later learned that a man in Lubbock, Texas, received Aaron's heart. A man in Houston, Texas, got one of his kidneys and a woman in Fort Worth, Texas, got his other kidney. We immediately began sending letters, cards and photographs through the hospital to the recipients because we wanted them to know something about Aaron and we wanted to know them and their families. For five years we sent letters and cards, but we never heard anything back.

Meanwhile, our family began to piece our lives back together. Margie and I became involved with MADD [Mothers Against Drunk Driving] and gave talks in local high schools. More than five years after Aaron's death we were invited to a high school near Lubbock, which made us again think of the man who had received Aaron's heart. We had continued to mail correspondence to reach him, but decided that this time we would contact the organ donation agency directly. I talked with the director and he assured me that if I sent something directly to the agency in Lubbock, he would personally see to it that it was given to the recipient. We composed a letter, mailed it off and waited.

Two weeks went by and we got a call from a man in Lubbock whose name we did not recognize. It turned out that he had found our letter in the middle of the road where it must have blown off a postal truck! He went to the trouble to let us know that he was forwarding it on to the addressee. I asked him if he'd read the letter and he said he had not. When we told him about its contents he was stunned.

A New Friendship

Eventually the letter made its way to Jack, the man who had received Aaron's heart. He and his wife Charlene were eager to meet us so we made arrangements to meet them in a public place. Our first visit lasted more than two hours. Jack and Charlene told us that they had wanted to find out about the heart's donor and his family, but were told that we had to make the first move. They had waited in vain for a communication from us. We later learned that the hospital never passed on our correspondence to any of the three recipients.

Despite the delay, they looked at all of the photos, videos and letters from teachers about Aaron that we brought. We gave them a large picture of Aaron along with copies of letters and other items. They invited us to their home to meet their oldest son and his family. When we arrived later that afternoon, we were very, very touched to see that they already had Aaron's picture in a frame on their coffee table. We watched videos of Aaron and laughed and cried.

Now Jack and Charlene had a name and face to add to their family and we had new members for our own. Before our visit was over, Jack and Charlene were referring to Aaron by his name. We could not have had a better visit; we came away relieved and pleased.

We invited Jack and his family to come to the high school presentation we were to do. When I introduced Jack to the students as the recipient of Aaron's heart; he was given a huge round of applause.

Aaron's Death Brought Strangers Together

Learning from our experience with Jack, we became assertive about meeting the other recipients. My wife and I met Bill just this year—the Houston man who got one of Aaron's kidneys. Our families spent Thanksgiving together and had a wonderful time. Since Bill's transplant he's earned his Masters degree, fathered two children and gotten a more fulfilling job. He now teaches at a small college in Houston.

Unfortunately, we were never able to meet the recipient of Aaron's other kidney. We learned that the woman experienced a delayed reaction and it had to be removed. She died of cancer just a few months ago.

We were eager to meet the recipients. It was important for us to know that they are good people and that Aaron's organs went to people who would care for them. We hoped that they are as caring and loving as he was. To meet and talk to the recipients was very emotional, but it's very comforting to know that Aaron is still around and still helping others.

As a result of our experiences, we've also helped the hospital involved renew its commitment to facilitating communications between donor families and recipients. In the future, other families like ours will have an easier time if they want to have those communications. We did not expect, but certainly welcomed, making Jack and Bill and their families part of our own. We recently spent a long weekend with Jack and Charlene and their daughter and family. Jack is doing great.

Aaron did not make it to his high school graduation. He did not get to attend college. He did not marry and father his own children. He did not have the opportunity to experience the future. But he lives on, not just in the minds and hearts of those who loved him, but very tangibly in Bill and Jack and in all they have done and become.

The Death of Steve Howe

Eric Olsen

Eric Olsen always identified strongly with troubled professional baseball player Steve Howe, who at age forty-eight died in a single-car accident. Like Howe, Olsen struggled for many years with alcohol abuse. He acknowledges in the following selection that he drove drunk many times, though he never hurt himself or others while doing so. One night, Olsen witnessed the afteref-fects of a fatal drunk driving accident when drunk himself, and he decided never to abuse alcohol again. In many ways, the au-thor uses the former pitcher as a mirror for his own life, though Olsen managed to turn his life around before causing irreparable harm. Olsen is a media professional and the founder and pub-lisher of Blogcritics.org.

Though I never met him, the death of former major league pitcher Steve Howe, 48, in an early morning, single ve-hicle, freeway accident in Southern California [in April 2006] hit me hard and low. I always thought of Howe—whose ca-reer as a left-handed closer began so promisingly as Rookie of the Year for the [Los Angeles] Dodgers in 1980 before stutter-ing then stalling out after *seven* suspensions for drugs and al-cohol—as sort of my vastly more talented doppelganger.

Howe was just a few months older than I; we were of similar size, and we were both left-handed pitchers. Though my career peaked in high school, Howe was the Dodgers' closer by the time he was 22. I always rooted for him to get his career, then his life, back together long after he became much better known as a bad joke and an embarrassment than as a sensational pitcher. I never gave up on the guy—perhaps because it would have felt like giving up on myself.

Eric Olsen, "The Death of Steve Howe," *BlogCritics Magazine*, May 2, 2006. http://blogcritics.org/archives/2006/05/02/113359.php. Reproduced by permission.

Driving Under the Influence

I too had my problems with substance abuse all through my late-teens and twenties. I can't believe I never hurt myself or anyone else given the *hundreds* of times I drove under the influence of alcohol over a period of about 15 years. The extent of my fortune and the severity of the consequences should my force field of luck falter, finally hit home on a late summer night in 1989.

For several years I had been telling myself that I was a better DJ when I drank—I relaxed, got into it more. I also got sloppy, ruined equipment and records, flirted with women I had no interest in, and said stupid things. But I could ignore that.

That night, my friend, the manager of a long-gone dance club carved out of the Sea Lion restaurant in Malibu [California], was going away to law school and I had just become separated from my first wife. So, for very different reasons, we raised many a glass together throughout the evening as I had entertained a gathering of tourists and locals while waves scenically danced against the break water and splashed upon the club's large picture windows.

Trying to Mask the Alcohol

With the drinking finally finished and the club closed, I brushed my teeth and scooped up a finger-full of peanut butter out of the jar I kept in the truck to mask the odor of alcohol. I chuckled at my own cleverness.

I wound my way south through the misty twists and turns of Pacific Coast Highway at 3:00 AM as it snaked down toward Sunset [Boulevard] with my brain buried under the sweet, humming insulation of too much alcohol.

Grinning vacantly, I took another hairpin turn at a reasonable but exhilarating speed and spied traffic cones ahead forcing me toward the center of the road. Oh bother.

I came to a near-stop behind several other cars just before the Sunset intersection. The cones ambiguously either wanted us to turn left onto Sunset or to continue south in the far left lane. Some cars turned onto Sunset, some went on ahead. I chose the second option.

Around another bend, frantic activity and grim faces in uniforms confirmed that we had made a mistake. At least I wasn't alone in my error. The night was lit hallucinogenically with ambulances and police cars flashing and clashing their garish, assaultive lights.

A few cars ahead, a figure waved emphatically for the line of cars to turn around. As I slowly backed to turn around, a blinding light shone in through my driver's window and a gruff knock followed. Startled, I stopped and rolled down my window.

"What the hell are you doing? Can't you follow directions? Don't back that way, you fool." An unexpected note of panic, or fear cut through the officer's voice.

Getting Arrested

I mumbled apologies and things about following other cars and this and that. The cop smiled and held his hand up for me to be silent.

"Have you been drinking peanut butter cocktails all night? I think you'll be spending the evening with us, buddy." The cop sounded strangely calm and almost kind. "Straighten this thing out and get out of the car."

I turned the truck so that it again faced south, my original direction. My headlights shone on the ambulance in front of me and on a long white, billowing object on the ground between my truck and the ambulance. A sudden wet gust up from the breakers blew the white covering off of the object, over the ambulance, and fluttering into the darkness.

Immediately before me was a red, blue and white object that, in a sickening jolt, I realized was a dead, male body. It—

he—was impossibly broken and naked except for socks and shoes. Mortified, I turned away. The officer and I stared at each other in silence.

The officer told me that the body was an 18 year-old kid who had been playing a perverse form of chicken with a buddy by mooning passing cars from the ocean side of the road. The competition had led each incrementally into the road itself.

I Was Lucky

A Porsche had come around the blind bend at 85 mph [miles per hour] and turned the kid into puree. The driver and the mooners had been drinking—just like I had. In that moment of horror, a calm certainty came over me that I had to stop drinking. I felt very lucky, very ill, and very guilty at the same time sitting there in police custody.

I don't take any particular credit for this decision—it didn't even feel like my decision to make. It felt like unavoidable received wisdom. Not that there aren't people who make the other choice, or who refuse to choose, which is the same thing. I stopped completely for about eight years, and have found over the last several years that I can drink lightly, not want more, and be okay; but I needed all of that time off for my body, brain and soul to recalibrate themselves into something resembling "normal."

The Fatal Accident

"For unknown reasons," a California Highway Patrol statement said, Howe's pickup truck—traveling westbound at about 70 mph at 5:30 AM, April 28 on Interstate 10 near Cactus City—left the roadway, entered the median and rolled numerous times before coming to rest on its roof. Howe was not wearing his seat belt and was partly ejected from the truck. He was pronounced dead at the scene. Results from toxicology tests have not yet been released. [Toxicology reports later showed that Howe had methamphetamine in his system.]

Dodger broadcaster Rick Monday, a former teammate of Howe's, told the *LA Times*, "He seemed to constantly struggle to figure out how to get his life in order. But no matter how bad things were, Steve always found a ray of sunshine."

The Scars of a Drunk Driving Accident Remain

Brian Reeder

In this essay, Brian Reeder recounts the experience of being in a car accident involving a drunk driver when he was in the sixth grade. In minute detail, he describes the emotions, sensation, and trauma of that night and reflects on the realization that he survived the accident to live a meaningful life. Brian Reeder is a writer who maintains a blog.

Years ago I was hit by a drunk driver on [state route] 99E between Canby and Oregon City, Oregon. I carry many emotional scars from the experience, and am still haunted by what I saw that day. As a twelve year old it was very difficult to understand why some things happen and deal with those very grown up issues. Pain, fear, hatred, and malice are all emotions that should be beyond a sixth grader's capacity. Unfortunately it seems that they are becoming the standard. This is my perspective, my story of the events.

A clay-brown blur was spinning. A harsh full lung scream was cut off by the louder sickly scream of metal-on-metal and breaking glass. A wave broke over me, enveloping me in noise, shock, and white. It seemed to last for hours but was over in a moment.

The noise was from the obvious. Two cars approaching at 70 and 85 miles an hour and striking each other head on will do that. The sound was harsh—a deep and soul-chilling boom combined with the screech of metal and the hiss of air.

The shock and white went together. The airbag (which saved my life) exploded—leaving a badly burned and confused boy. This happens in a very small number of cases, less than 1% from what I could gather. As a result, the chemicals which inflate the bag were released straight onto my face. It was like I had a rug burn from my sternum to my upper lip. I felt it but my fingers didn't take away any blood.

Chemicals will do that, especially, while they're still burning through layers of skin.

It Was My Friend's Birthday

I turned to see about my three friends in the back seat. As I looked left I saw Andrew lodged between me and the driver. He was sitting in the back of the Jeep Grand Cherokee. The very back. Luckily his weight protected him [from] any serious injury. I guess he should get lucky—it was his birthday party we were going to. His mother was also lucky physically, but I can't imagine the guilt of driving into a fatal accident with your son and four other boys in your care. It was in no way her fault.

My three friends in the back seat weren't as lucky. Blake was grey and limp. His head rested on Lane's shoulder, I could see his face swell in front of me. Lane was rubbing his shoulder, stating matter-of-factly that his collarbone was broken. Blake must have a hard face.

Mark just looked bad. He was shaking visibly and looking around bewildered. I can't imagine what I looked like. I couldn't feel. I couldn't think. But I could move. I asked Glenda (the mother) politely if I could get out of the car. She affirmed, and I wrestled the front door open and staggered onto the pavement. More the shoulder, the speed of the impact pushed our car two lanes over. Better than [the other driver's] ... car—it was in two pieces 40 yards apart. Fear gripped every sense I possessed. I couldn't feel. I could only move. I walked around the car.

Mark and Lane were standing and staring. Blood. Bile. Shock.

Time Seemed to Slow Down

I'm glad I couldn't feel. It would have been too much. Sinew was all that kept head to body. Sickness. I was swimming, over the hot asphalt. Walking with purpose. Get away. I was led to a car. Sat down. Front seat again—I wanted out. Someone told me it was ok. I believed them. I was handed a phone. I put it aside to look in the vanity mirror. Someone tried to stop me. I had to. Not much vanity there. I was no longer swimming, but floating. I could only see Blake's face. . . . Never to move again, Blake would.

A blood alcohol level of .30 will sometimes kill a man. Sometimes it will cause him to kill. [The drunk driver] . . . probably didn't feel a thing. Just a deep resonating boom— then nothing.

Now a phone call. My mother's receptionist. Then my father. Then another hand. Out of the car, into an ambulance. Still no feeling. Just automatic, needed, forced movement. Instructions—do this, move that, feel this. I don't want to feel. Just move. Pain. Refreshingly sharp and concentrated. Easy almost. Comforting. I loved it because I could feel. Unlike him [the drunk driver].

Wrists, nose, jaw, face. All battered. Burnt. Numbness everywhere else. I wanted to feel. Emotions. Something.

The hospital, and my mother. Glass everywhere. Slow, deliberate movement. Comfort in her touch. In safety.

Eventual movement. A familiar car. And then the flood. Of knowledge, of emotion, of feeling. I had felt the physical pain, I had no idea how much worse the mental torment would be. Blinding, panicked fear. Every moment.

The impact was a wave, quick to recede and never to return.

The fallout was an ocean, vast beyond compare and impossible to understand.

This accident changed my life. I grew up more than I already had. I understood what I had been given in life. That I had life. I vowed that night never to waste a day of it. I pray I never will.

A Mother Forgives the Driver Who Took Her Daughter's Life

Joyce Bries

In this selection, the author describes the violent death of her daughter Debbie and how her family was shaken by the loss. Joyce Bries also recounts her renewed faith in God and her awareness that her daughter will always be with her. Even though the drunk driver shows no remorse, she finds it in herself to forgive him because he did not intend to kill her daughter.

Grief is something we all experience at some time in our lives. My first experience was at the age of 8 when my mom died. She was only 49. My father came home from the hospital and said, "Mommy is dead. None of you will shed a tear or you won't go to the funeral." My father, 14 years older than Mom, was a strict old-fashioned German. For one year after Mom's death we kids were only allowed to go to school or church, and nowhere else. We were not allowed to say anything about her being gone. My oldest sister, at 18, took over as our mother the best she could. For the rest of my life I have heard the refrain "Big girls don't cry" in my head. Although it has colored my existence, I had to learn through experience that it wasn't true.

My husband Arnie and I married in 1971. We have been blessed with six children—two sons and four daughters. Debbie is our third child. She always had a bubbly personality, a ready smile, and mischief in her green eyes.

Joyce Bries, "Big Girls Do Cry," *Suffering: The Stauros Notebook*, vol. 23, Autumn 2004. www.stauros.org/notebooks/. Copyright © 2004 by Stauros U.S.A. Reproduced by permission.

Mother and Daughter Working Together

Debbie and I worked together at one of the restaurants in our rural Iowa town. We both enjoyed being co-workers, viewing each other in a different dimension than as mother and daughter. One June day in 1993 we were headed to work to help serve a funeral dinner. I remarked to Debbie that when my Mom died we were "housebound" for one year. She thought that was "dumb." I told her it was the custom at the time, and added, "I don't know what I'd do if I lost you or anyone else in our family." She replied, "If you died Mom, I'd miss you but life goes on." I again stated I didn't know if I'd be able to cope should one of my kids die. Her comeback was, "Well if I die and you think you're just gonna sit around and cry, I'm gonna come and kick you in the ass!" We both laughed and then went on to other subjects.

Debbie, an incoming junior, was the starting shortstop for the high school softball team and was well known for her on-the-field chatter. Many days she'd dash into the house and fly upstairs shouting, "Mom! Is my uniform clean? Got a game! You coming? See you there!" And off she'd go to pick up Carie, her close friend and classmate who was the starting catcher. The girls had played softball together for over 10 years and had a lot of fun.

Watching the Girls Play

July began with Carie's mom and me sitting together in the stands watching our girls play ball. Afterwards the girls could hardly contain themselves as they plotted their agenda for a trip to Georgia with Carie's family to see an Atlanta Braves [baseball] game. The next day, Arnie and I left with the three younger kids, Bill, Katie, and Lynn, for a two-day vacation to Minnesota to visit good friends. Amy and Deb were staying home over the 4th of July, and Brian was in Iowa City for the summer.

We arrived at Steve and Darlene's house by 8:00 and spent the evening playing cards and visiting. It was almost 1:00 when we got to bed. I heard the phone ring at 1:15. Darlene came downstairs and said it was for us. When I took the phone, the voice at the other end said she was a nurse at our local hospital. She asked if Deborah Sue Bries was my daughter. I said she was and whispered a quick prayer asking God to not let her be paralyzed. Then as if in a fog I heard the nurse say, "I'm sorry to inform you that Debbie was killed in a car accident earlier this evening." The world stopped and yet went into overdrive at the same time. Amy, What about Amy? The nurse put Amy on the line. At first all she could say was "I'm sorry Mom. Debbie's dead." She hadn't been in the car with Deb and she didn't know what happened other than that four other kids were in the car, Deb was driving, and a truck hit them head-on. Amy didn't know how the other kids were. She didn't know what Deb's injuries were. She didn't know the cause of the accident. There were so many questions, and so few answers.

Terrible News

When we hung up the phone I collapsed into Arnie's arms and cried. Bill came into the room and Arnie had to tell him his sister was dead. More tears. More disbelief. How could this be happening? We decided to drive back home immediately, but we wanted to let Katie and Lynn sleep until morning. Darlene promised to break the news to them gently and to drive back with them as soon as they could pack up and go. The drive home was somber. Bill cried himself to sleep. Arnie kept saying to me, "Pray it was not her fault." We decided on classmates for pallbearers and the softball team as honorary pallbearers. How could we even be thinking of these things?

Friendliness of Strangers

I had to stop for a bathroom, but nothing was open at that hour. There were lights on at the police station in one small town, and we stopped there. I told the officer our daughter was killed in an accident, we were driving home to her, and I had to use the facilities. When I came back out, the officers gave us coffee and donuts to take along. It's amazing how compassionate strangers can be.

When we arrived home about 7:15, Brian and his girl-friend Maria were just arriving from Iowa City. People began coming to the house with condolences and food. We were told that one other boy, Randy, died in the accident. Arnie fried some eggs but I couldn't eat. We spent the day making funeral arrangements, choosing readings, asking people to serve as ministers or pallbearers, and bringing clothes for Deb to be buried in (the funeral director specified a shirt with a high collar and long sleeves). It all seemed so surreal. I waited to wake up from this nightmare.

Back at home I hid out in the kitchen. I appreciated the people but I didn't want to talk to them. When Katie and Lynn arrived home, everyone graciously left us alone. We held each other and cried for a very long time. That evening we went to Randy's home to talk with his parents. It was an emotional meeting. They told us the highway patrol assured them it was not Debbie's fault—that the truck had crossed the line and hit them while they were fully in their lane. He said Deb never had a chance. Thank God.

A Public Viewing

The next afternoon we went to the funeral home to view Debbie's body before the public came. I touched her arm and it crinkled, the sleeve stuffed with tissue paper. I didn't touch her again. The wake and funeral were packed with people— our little girl was well loved. I told Arnie my heart actually hurt. How could I say goodbye?

Back at home after the funeral, Arnie and I talked about the stories we'd heard where a child's death breaks up a marriage. We vowed to each other and to God not to let that happen to us. We had lost our daughter; we did not want to lose each other too. We also talked with the kids and told them we had a choice. We could be mad that Debbie died, or we could be glad we had her in our lives as long as we did and have faith that she was happy in heaven with God. We knew there would be many times of sadness and many tears, and that is OK too; we had to learn to live without Deb's presence in our home. Yet Deb would always be part of our family, and after all, if we all just sat around and cried she was going to come and kick our collective ass!

Shedding Tears Openly

Over the next couple of days, Brian went back to his apartment. Arnie went back to work. I took my daycare kids back. Life went on. The kids seemed to sense when I was down, and six pairs of little arms surrounded me. Sometimes they would be playing and they'd start talking about Debbie. "Yup," they'd say, "we can't see Deb no more but she's still here!" They didn't hide their thoughts of Deb, and would often keep talking until I started to smile at the memories, even if through tears. These kids were my therapy group. I found that tears came readily, both when I was sad and when I was happy, or sometimes when I experienced both emotions at once. Big girls do cry after all.

In October as I was sleeping one night I felt a presence near me. A voice said, "Deb's going to call. You can talk to her but you can't tell her she's dead." I heard the phone ring and I answered it. "Hi Mom, it's Deb." I replied, "Oh Debbie how are you?" She bubbled over about how beautiful it was there, that it was almost unbelievable. She asked whether the farmers were picking corn yet, whether Brian was back at his job and Amy at school, and if her favorite daycare child was talking yet. Then she said she missed us but she had to go. She asked to talk to Arnie, so I told her I loved her and I missed her, then set the phone down to get Arnie. That's when

I woke up. I felt like my "conversation" with Deb was a gift from God. I felt peaceful and assured.

Over time more information came out about the accident. The man who killed Deb and Randy had a blood alcohol level of .21—over twice the legal limit. When the kids got into the car Deb had insisted everyone put on their seat belts before she would shift into drive—an act that saved more lives from being lost. Still, the list of injuries was long. Deb died instantly, crushed from shoulder to ankle. Carie had a broken back and facial cuts. One boy in the rear seat had a broken pelvis and broken bones in his face. Michael had a broken leg, broken pelvis, and glass cuts. Randy had a broken pelvis, too, and died two hours after the accident from a ruptured aorta. The drunk driver of the pickup truck suffered only a broken leg.

Driver Shows No Remorse

The ensuing trial was extremely difficult. It was almost too much to take when the driver tried to evade responsibility by petitioning to have the blood alcohol limit thrown out as evidence. When the judge refused, the man pled. "No contest." In other words, he wouldn't say he was innocent, but he wouldn't admit guilt either. It also meant that although the judge heard the test results, he did not hear any other evidence that would have been presented in the trial.

At the sentencing, we were not allowed to make any statements as it would be "upsetting to the defendant." His sentence was 12 years each on the two vehicular homicide charges and 2 years each for bodily harm to the other three kids. Since the sentences were served concurrently and he would benefit from provisions for behavior, he would be out of prison in 6 years. The families were devastated, knowing he had been free already for six months before the trial, he would be free for six more weeks before he started serving, and for all the devastation he caused he would be in jail only six years. The families then served lawsuits on the two taverns at which he had purchased alcohol that day. We were successful in both, and felt that at least we made an impact on how liquor was served in the county.

The driver was granted a parole hearing in 1999. Three of the families spoke at his parole hearing. He showed no remorse or accountability, and was denied, parole. However, he was released from prison in January of 2000.

Achieving Forgiveness

It took a long time and a lot of soul-searching, but I have forgiven the driver. Despite his irresponsibility, it was indeed an accident. No one gets into their car intending to kill and injure kids. I found that if I hate someone (as I did indeed hate him at first) it colors my whole world and everything in it. Nothing is good. Nothing is peaceful. I prayed that God would help me forgive as I hoped to be forgiven when I did wrong. I prayed for acceptance of Deb's death, not as something God caused but as something that happened. I prayed to know that Deb attained eternal happiness in heaven with God, something we all hope to attain some day. Eventually, although I am still not happy that Deb can't be with us in this life, I accepted the fact that she died, I accepted the fact that this was a tragic accident, and I forgave the driver. I am free.

I've learned that no two people grieve the same. Grief is very personal; there is no "right" or "wrong" way. I wanted details of the accident and Arnie did not. I never shared the information I learned from the highway patrol and EMT's [emergency medical technicians] because I knew it would cause him too much pain. We did not and do not miss Debbie in the same ways but we both miss her. Just as we love our children differently, we grieve them differently when they are gone.

Amy needed to find a way to bring life back into her world. She began dating a friend of Deb's boyfriend who came to the wake. A few months later, she announced her pregnancy and Tyler was born about a year after Deb died. Amy and Travis got married, and now also have a daughter to add to the family. Amy's kids know Aunt Debbie loves them and watches over them.

Missing the Dead

Amy and I talk of Debbie and our memories of her; the other four kids don't as much. Yet Brian and Bill both married and have children, and they are already teaching the kids about their special Aunt Debbie. Katie just got married and made sure Deb's favorite song was played at their wedding dance. Lynn, who was only eight when Debbie died, regrets that she didn't know her better. I tell her to listen in the silence, and Deb may still be teaching her and imparting some big-sister wisdom.

I now talk to the area high school students on the danger of drinking and driving. I don't believe I can make them not drink, but I pray they will not drive drunk. I also talk at meetings of people with multiple violations for driving under the influence. I ask them to plan a way home other than driving before they even take the first drink. I ask them how they would feel if they had to live with the knowledge that they killed someone. I ask them to throw away the extra keys they have hidden on their vehicle, keys they know will be accessible in case someone takes their set away from them. I ask them never to be the cause of another person's heartbreak.

I am the mother of six children, but one of them resides in heaven. I know when someone else I love dies, I will grieve differently for them than I have for Deb. But I know God gives me the grace and strength to handle whatever happens. I know God cares for me and my family. I know God lost a son to death and understands the pain and hurt I feel. We thank God for allowing us to have Deb in our family and to have known her love. We would not have changed having her even

37

had we known the pain we'd endure. Debbie's soul is in heaven, but her memory and spirit in us will never die.

Taking Responsibility for Oneself and Others

Crystal Sciarini

*Recounting her own tragic experience with a drunk driving inci-
dent, the author asks why drunk driving still has not been eradicated. She comes to the conclusion that people have to take responsibility for their own actions and decisions if they do not
want to hurt innocent strangers. She also encourages the public
to not let friends and colleagues drive while intoxicated.*

April 7, 1997, is a night I will never forget. The night played
out in slow motion and every moment is seared into my
brain forever. I got the call at 9:07 PM. My sister calls to tell
me that Mom just called her [and told her that] Dean, our
step dad, has been in a four car accident.

"I'm not sure how he is, but, it was bad. He is at Froedert
[hospital], meet us there."

I woke up my 2 1/2 year old son and shakily got him
ready to go I fought back tears, while I sped towards the freeway on ramp. A ten minute drive was delayed by construction
and through tears I screamed at the cars around me to get out
of my way. Unfortunately, my tantrums disturbed my son and
he also began to wail. In a strange way it was comforting.
Forty five minutes later I quickly slammed the car into park
and ran into the ER [emergency room] waiting room.

The Story of an Accident

I was amazed to find the entire family already present along
with our Pastor and some church friends. As we waited for
word from beyond the double doors the story of Dean's night
began to unfold.

Crystal Sciarini, "How Drunk Driving Changed My Life," *Associated Content*, February
5, 2007. www.associatedcontent.com. Reproduced by permission.

My dad was on his way to a funeral driving down HWY [highway] 32 in Muskego. WI HWY [Wisconsin highway] 32 at that time was a two lane undivided highway. He must have [seen] the oncoming car swerving, because he pulled to the shoulder of the road as far as he could maneuver his truck without rolling into the ditch. The two cars behind him followed suit. Within moments all three stationary cars were in the ditch. Dean's truck had taken the brunt of the damage. His truck was hit at an estimated 70 miles an hour head on into the front quarter panel. Even though Dean was wearing his seat belt he was thrown from the truck when the latch was demolished upon impact.

"Is everyone alright?" that's what Dean kept asking as the passengers of the two cars behind him came to his aid. That shows you what kind of a person he was. As he lay dying on the side of the road, his concern was not for himself. He continued to repeat his question as those aiding him reassured him that help was on the way.

The police arrived just moments after the accident. A driver behind the swerving car had called 911 and reported the erratic driver. The police were already positioning to intercept the reported driver when the calls started coming in that there had been an accident.

Back in the waiting room [we were] encouraged that Dean [had still been] alive when transported and thankful that the elderly couple in the car directly behind Dean's in the accident had made the effort to come to the ER and share their story and their concern for Dean with us.

Dean Did Not Survive the Accident

Within minutes of my arrival the double doors opened and an unsmiling face approached our large group "I'm sorry, Dean did not survive. Dean is available for anyone who would like to see him." The family all began to gather around Dean's body, but the moment I saw him my stomach [turned] and I ran for the bathroom. A kind nurse followed me into the bathroom and made sure I was ok while I could swear I was puking up everything I had ever eaten in my 22 years. I did manage to make it back to the [emergency] room and spent a few minutes with the family before they gently reminded us that they would need to move his body soon.

My husband was out of town and I did not want to spend the night alone so I slept on my sister's couch. I am sure we all hoped we would wake up to find that the night before had been a dream. The next few days are a blur. I vaguely remember sitting next to my Mom at the funeral home while plans were made to lay Dean to rest and being interviewed by a few TV stations that had picked up the story. I don't remember the moment that I learned that the crash was caused by a drunk driver or when I learned the drunk driver's name.

The Crash Was Caused by a Drunk Driver

Jimmy Lee Kennedy. That is the name of the man that changed my life. During the court hearings over the next few months I just wanted to scream at Jimmy Lee Kennedy. *Why?* Why would you jeopardize your life? Didn't you think about your daughters? Do you really feel remorseful?

Jimmy Lee Kennedy, a repeat drunk driver, you changed our lives forever. You changed *your* life forever.

Drunk driving, why is drunk driving even an issue? We have cabs, buses, designated driver programs, but most of all we have common sense Don't we? Here is a societal problem that is 100% preventable! One hundred percent, people. If you drink, don't drive. It is as easy as that. Just don't do it.

This year, 2007, will be the tenth "anniversary" of Dean's death. Ten years have come and gone. Dean's grandchildren are now 16, 12, 11, and 9. Yes, nine, just weeks after the murder my sister found out she was pregnant. For Dean's anniversary I just want one thing: no drunk driving. I want to wake up into a world where no one would even think about drinking and driving. A world where friends don't let friends drive drunk, where bartenders and bouncers take responsibility for the condition of their customers who are walking out their doors with keys in hand.

Do you think if I close my eyes tight and click my heels three times my wish will come true? Maybe it's not that easy, but it can happen and it starts with you.

CHAPTER 2

I Drunk Drivers Speak Out

I Feel Ashamed for Driving Under the Influence

Superdork

In this article, the author wonders who the drunk drivers—often demonized by the media—are, and she suggests that most of them are just regular people, their judgment temporarily impaired. Confessing to driving drunk and accumulating a long history of alcoholism, the author describes her own self-absorption when under the influence, and concludes that alcohol changes moral judgments and leads to a temporary impairment of reason.

When we hear of incidents where unsuspecting motorists in the wrong place at the wrong time are victims of someone's irresponsible and deadly decision to drive drunk, it incites sorrow and anger in us. Sometimes a whole family is wiped out at once, while the perpetrating drunk walks away with barely a scratch. How much of an injustice is this? We want stiff penalties for such senseless and atrocious offenses, rightfully so.

Well, who are these offenders? Are they mean and dangerous people who don't care if they kill others? Sometimes. But a lot of the time they are people just like anyone else, [but with] one monumental defect: extreme self-absorption.

I spent 12 years as a desperate and miserable alcoholic, 8 of those years as a driver, and will reveal here my past shameful experience as a regular drunk driver.

A Series of Bad Decisions

There are questions reasonable people would want a drunk driver to answer. I will do my best to answer them and offer insight into the mind of someone who has made this bad decision repeatedly.

Superdork, "Confessions of a Drunk Driver: Selfishness, Sickness and Shame: What Are Drunk Drivers Really Thinking?," *Associated Content*, February 14, 2007. www.assoc iatedcontent.com. Reproduced by permission.

How did it ever come to be that you thought it was okay to get behind the wheel in this condition and endanger lives?

I never thought drunk driving was okay when I was sober, only when I was drunk. At those times I only cared about the fact that I wanted to get from point A to point B. I didn't want to surrender my car and my perceived control, or be at the mercy of anyone else. I say perceived control because when drunk it can feel like you are totally in control, when in fact that could not be further from the truth. The reasoning ability I'd have before would be compromised more with each drink.

How many DWIs [driving while intoxicated citations] have you gotten and how many accidents have you been involved in?

In all the years and times I drove drunk, somehow I never had an accident and never got a DWI. There were two different times that I was pulled over extremely drunk, minutes after leaving the bar at closing time. One of the times I was going 75 in a 45mph [miles per hour] zone. The officer wrote me a ticket, but never even questioned whether or not I had been drinking, even though I had been—for more than 7 hours.

Another time I was pulled over drunk, I had been having a hard time keeping my eyes open. I already had to drive with one eye open, and I was of course speeding. I had expired inspection and registration stickers, no insurance and was extremely intoxicated after hours of drinking. This time an officer let me off with a warning for all my violations, and did not even ask me if I'd been drinking. In both instances I would have flunked a field sobriety test miserably.

There were also countless times where I drove from one location to the other with no recollection of doing so. I don't know how I did not kill someone or myself, or get any DWIs. I don't know what would have changed if those things had happened. I was a pretty hopeless case during those years.

Extreme Self-Absorption

It seems that in this lifestyle, a pattern of behavior emerges. Why then couldn't you predict future behavior based on past behavior, and make adjustments accordingly? Couldn't you, when sober, have planned for the fact ahead of time that you would be drunk at the end of the night and believe you could drive since that's what always happened before?

This is where the extreme self-absorption comes into play. When someone is deep in the throes of alcoholism, so much of their physiology is damaged. People in this condition function as someone 15–20 years younger than their age. They throw temper tantrums when they don't get their way, they screw over people they love without even blinking and the only thing that matters to them is making each of their moments as tolerable as possible. This is where I was during these years. Nothing in my thought process was ever about doing what would be best for someone else. If it infringed even slightly on my selfish agenda, it was not up for consideration.

People don't realize how much alcoholism attacks the very character and value of a person. It makes them nothing more than a burden to those around them, and a menace to society. I am so ashamed that I behaved this way for so long. It is not who I was before, and not who I am today.

Now that you have children, how hard has it been to reconcile that for years you put other people's children in danger on a regular basis?

Today I have been sober for 7 years, and it is painful to remember the things I did before. Much of the time I do not like to be out at night, especially not with my family in the car, because I know there are "old me"s out there. I am afraid for my family to drive out of town for a trip.

I imagine the scenario of us, this family minding our own business, getting destroyed out of nowhere by some irresponsible idiot. I think of the rage I would have if one of those people caused me to lose one of my most valued treasures, and what I would want to do to them. Every time I see this happen to someone else, my blood starts to boil, and I feel hatred for the drunk driver.

Then I remember that I used to be one of them, and that the only difference between them and me is that I just happen to never [have] hit anyone.

It Is Hard to Find a Cure

Perhaps as long as there is alcoholism, there will be drunk driving. And as long as there is drunk driving, innocent people will die. It's hard to implement a program that makes changes to a person's heart. That's what ultimately led to my transformation and brought an end to this destructive behavior.

Nothing short of a miracle made me stop being what I was. I was so enslaved to this stronghold that it felt impossible to ever do anything different. I am so glad that was a lie and that I can live.

There are never any excuses for driving drunk. It doesn't make sense to so many of us. That is because it is senseless. At least with my change there is one fewer drunk driver out there. Here's to hoping many more will make the same changes, and escape this insane way of life without killing someone.

My Excessive Lifestyle Threatened to Destroy Me and Others

Joe Plummer

In this personal history, Joe Plummer recalls early drug and alcohol addiction, which ultimately led to increasingly self-destructive behavior. Even after beating an addiction to illegal drugs, his continued alcohol consumption resulted in four citations for driving under the influence (DUI), carrying a possible penalty of up to two years in prison. Finally, after another drunk driving incident he decided to sober up and reject alcohol for good.

My name is Joe Plummer. I'm not a clinical psychologist or an MD [medical doctor] with an Ivy League education. I'm simply a man who over a period of many years grew tired of my life and my apparent inability to effectively change it. Substances (this includes alcohol) had become a primary source of avoidable problems and pain. Through trial and error I eventually realized any contact with them brought a predictable result: more problems and pain. Although this was easy enough to see, the issue of how to actually tackle the problem was not.

My drug use began at what many would consider a very young age. I was 9 years old when my babysitter and her older brother first introduced me to marijuana. They were probably 13 and 16 (respectively) and were very much into the teenage "drug lifestyle." As a result, I learned fast what "partying" was all about from the two of them and their older friends. I suppose you could say, because there were no others, they became my role models. (Not a good choice on my part—but hey, we all make mistakes, right?)

Joe Plummer, "My Background," StopDrinking.com. Accessed online August 25, 2007, at www.stopdrinking.com.

I Was Cool

Because nobody had ever warned me about drugs and alcohol (not many knew the dangers themselves back then, let alone knew enough to warn a 9 year old) I never questioned a thing my new role models taught me. Drugs were what cool people did and I was cool! I lived and breathed this new and exciting way of life as fully as I could. Although my drug of choice was marijuana, I experimented with other drugs like hash, opium, speed, acid, and cocaine. Drinking was also a big part of the equation but again, pot was what I used most.

At the time (and even now) everyone looked at marijuana as basically a "harmless/passive" drug. I guess to some extent that observation is true. Unfortunately, when words like "responsibility" or "moderation" haven't even entered your vocabulary (let alone become concepts you actually understand) pot can easily turn you into a passive person interested in little more than getting high. I spent so much of my time high, I probably didn't make a sensible decision from age 9 until I was finally incarcerated at age 15. (It's no mystery you make a lot of mistakes while under the influence of drugs and alcohol and I made too many to list.)

Within a few months of making my new lifestyle choice, I began stealing. It was nothing major; but a step in the wrong direction nonetheless. My older friends would distract the owner at the local wine store while I lifted a bottle (or two) of MD 20/20 [wine with a high alcohol content]. After getting literally "puke drunk," we'd go out and do all kinds of illegal stuff like break into cars, vandalize, etc. . . .

I Was Too Far Gone

Life consisted of: Get high before school, cause as much chaos as possible during school, cut for lunch, get high, go back for the last few periods; throw all my books in my locker, meet up with my friends, party some more and figure out where to get money so I could (you guessed it) buy some weed and get high. For years, I scammed and stole and sold drugs to support my habit and along with my behavior, my life began to deteriorate rapidly. I'd gone from scoring in the upper 92% of kids my age on the brain sheets to a zero point grade average. My behavior at school was unacceptable (to say the least) and the severity and frequency of my illegal activity had gotten pretty ugly. Unfortunately, by the time anyone noticed that I had a problem, I was too far gone.

My mother attempted (twice) to straighten me out by forcing me into treatment, but I wasn't hearing any of it. I defended my lifestyle to the death and was thrown out both times for being a serious pain in the ass. Drugs and alcohol were all I knew. They were part of a lifestyle I'd sworn my allegiance to. They were, in a very real sense, a huge part of who I was.

When the counselors would say I was "on a one way street to either jail or death" I would just laugh. My theory was: "If these idiots could predict the future, they wouldn't be working a crappy job like this." I felt it was my life and nobody had any right to tell me how to live it. I couldn't understand why everyone insisted on poking their nose where it didn't belong. Why couldn't they just leave me alone?

Of course, I now know it was my unacceptable behavior that prompted the ever-increasing instances of "intervention," but I was in such a fog at the time, I couldn't see that if I tried. The constant pressure on me to "stop using" only drove me further in the other direction; it only strengthened my bond with those who embraced and encouraged my lifestyle. I really was on a one way street and, as predicted, it ended at one of the predetermined destinations.

Although I'd been to court for a few other things prior, it was my third felony conviction in 1985 (at the age of 15) that brought my first real jail time. The saying "three strikes and you're out" fit perfectly. My Judge was a woman and I think, in her eyes, I'd finally done something there was no sweet-talking my way out of. I stole $1,200 cash from my Mom. "Her honor" expressed her displeasure in no uncertain terms. She handed down a 1 to 6 year sentence to be served in a notoriously nasty "21 and under" felony detention center. Damn right I was scared, but it was too late for that. . . .

Trading One Dependency for Another

By the time I was released from jail (I served 9 months total) I'd so thoroughly associated pot with everything I'd ever hated about myself or my life, the thought of "getting high" was nearly enough to make me gag. Where it once meant "cool" it now meant "stupid." Where it once meant "fun" it now meant "waste of life." Where it once meant "who I am" it now meant "who I have no desire to be." It was the first time I'd ever destroyed my desire to do something (more on that later) and it really did the trick. . . .

Abstaining from pot brought about many productive changes in my life. I managed to go from being a 115 lb lying, scamming, thieving dirtbag to a fairly trustworthy, physically improved (better diet + regular weight lifting) reasonably honest young adult with at least somewhat of a plan. Unfortunately for me and those around me, alcohol was part of that plan.

Although I'd sworn off weed, I hadn't thought much about what drinking could do to my life. (Maybe because I was too focused on what weed had done.) I guess you could say I substituted alcohol for pot, but not completely. I'd spent every waking moment of my life for years stoned; with the booze it was more or less a weekend thing. And thank God for that, because it was truly amazing how much trouble I could get in over the weekend. . . .

So, to briefly sum up 1986–1991, I was basically your average everyday guy who had stopped doing drugs but still drank on the weekends. I had a few high roller visions of grandeur about dealing that I eventually outgrew. The one glaring difference between me and the average everyday guy was: when I drank I had a tendency to turn into a completely psychotic moron capable of just about anything.

A Destructive Habit

As if you couldn't have guessed, it was just a matter of time before I was once again viewing the world from the confines of a jail cell; this time for my drinking extravaganzas. My highlight reel included things like: Breaking into a closed pizza shop to make myself dinner. Standing in the backyard of my "suburban subdivision" home with a .38 revolver; repeatedly loading and unloading it into the ground. Kicking out arresting officers' back windows, intentionally cutting myself with razors, knives or broken glass to watch myself bleed; fighting, shouting, acting like a complete idiot and racking up more driving violations than most families do in a lifetime. (I think I have 75 entries to date.)

Needless to say, things were not going too good and being the logical fast learning man I was (yeah right) it only took me about 5 years to figure out that alcohol was causing me just as much grief as pot had and, once again, I was looking at spending a lot of boring time behind bars. Different charges; same result.

On March 25th, 1991, I was cited with my fourth D.U.I. It carried a penalty of up to two years in jail. Three days later, drunk out of my mind, I decided I didn't like "no parking" signs. My solution was to spend a few hours driving around with a friend of mine running them down. (Fortunately, I did not get caught or I surely would have been cited for my fifth D.U.I. among other things.)

For me, March 28th, 1991, was the final straw. Here I was still facing up to two years in jail for my fourth D.U.I. [driving under the influence citation] on the 25th and I'm out (just a few days later) drunk and driving *and* intentionally running over street signs. When I woke up the next morning, my inner dialogue went something like this: "What are you, a f---ing idiot? Do you want to destroy yourself? Are you actually trying to ruin your life? Is this all you expect of yourself? Are you willing to accept this?"

It was that last question that really hit home. It reminded me of what I'd done to myself with other substances and the subsequent unacceptable behavior. The answer was an unequivocal "*no.*" Again, I was disgusted with the choices I'd made and concluded: "Screw this shit, it sucks, it's ruining my life. . . . I'm done." And I meant it.

Trying to Quit

OK, I'd made up my mind. Now it was time to deal with the social attitude that I couldn't just quit drinking without help from AA [Alcoholics Anonymous] and the program. You'd think my prior success in quitting drugs (despite having been given the same doom and gloom story) might have won me some confidence from the "well intentioned" masses . . . not a chance. Seems they figured I'd just substituted booze for drugs, so my accomplishment in that department (and other subsequent improvements) didn't really count. Even my friends who'd seen me stop smoking cigarettes, pot, doing coke, etc. didn't really believe in me.

Well, I'd been through "the program" many times (during in-patient treatment, and as punishment for each of my prior D.U.I.'s). If I was absolutely sure of anything it was this: The Program was not my cup of coffee. I hated the principles, procedures, pity, steps, prayers . . . basically everything about it. In short, I could not honestly force myself to believe that I was "powerless" over something that I was physically CHOOSING to do! It just didn't feel right to me. At best, it came off as a flimsy crutch; at worst, a potentially dangerous and debilitating belief system.

If I was going to stop drinking, I wasn't going to do it using "techniques" I didn't believe in. Like I had quit smoking cigarettes, quit doing coke, quit smoking pot (quit lying, quit stealing, etc.) I wanted to uncover and destroy the self-destructive thought processes that were driving my unacceptable behavior. I wanted to replace them with (for lack of a better term) "self-productive" thoughts and actions. And despite the naysayers (with their cynical/mocking tone still ringing in my ears) that is exactly what I did. I found what I'd hoped all along I would: It's easy to trade a bad life for a better one as long as you realize that is what you're doing. . . .

It Is Everyone's Choice

I remember specifically the challenges of my first week, month, & year sober . . . Of course there was a little fear! According to popular belief, the odds were stacked against me. Fortunately, I was able to determine what triggered my thoughts to drink during those early stages. The pattern was pretty obvious: Whenever I engaged in any activity or encountered any kind of stress that before would have included alcohol, my habitual thought was again to include alcohol . . . kind of like when you pick up your toothbrush, your habitual thought is to begin looking for the toothpaste. My first "sober" night in a bar, my first date, my first dinner at a fancy restaurant, my first boring weeknight, etc.—each of these prompted the habitual thought of "where is the beer?"

Recognizing this pattern helped me a lot. Where once I would have believed I had a merciless broken record in my head, randomly playing "You want to drink, you want to drink, you want to drink," I realized it was simply my mind following an established "sequence" that I had set up years ago. By the second, third, and fourth time I faced each activity without alcohol; I noticed the "new sequence" taking hold. (Walk into a bar, order a bottled water, sit down at a restaurant, order an iced tea, etc.)

Many people are nervous when they decide to stop drinking and doing drugs because they are afraid of the way they'll feel if they "can't" stop. They feel it will further affirm their inability to control themselves, or "prove" that they are an "addict." I say this is absolute nonsense.

All it will prove if you should decide to drink or do drugs is that you are still more comfortable with the struggle you've known with them, than the struggle of developing new strength. Rest assured, I "quit" drinking and doing drugs many times before I actually stopped.

What I say to everybody is this: If you feel like drinking, then drink. If you feel like doing drugs, they're everywhere, help yourself. Take mental notes, question how you feel, hold yourself accountable for the decision and *learn* something from it. I don't believe you should ever stop doing anything that you feel is really important to your life, but by the same token, if it seems to have become a total waste, then stop and take a couple more steps in the right direction. . . .

Trust in Oneself

After a short while you will begin to trust in your ability to make the right decisions. Don't be afraid of the question: "What if I start drinking again?" Who cares? It's your decision, you're an adult. Just say to yourself when that question comes to your mind, "Hey if that's what I decide to do someday, then it's my choice."

The bottom line here is, drugs and alcohol ain't goin' nowhere and membership to the club is real easy to get. Don't stop because you feel you must. That takes all the fun out of it. Stop because you want to. Remember: Only one mind can stop you from your goals in life, and that mind is yours. Understand and use this truth, no matter what the goal.

Earlier I stated: "It's easy to trade a bad life for a better one as long as you realize that is what you're doing." Some might wonder if the word "easy" is an exaggeration. It's not. In closing, I hope the following letter will provide some valuable insight into how "not drinking" can be easy—

even for those who (like myself) struggled to stop many times before we finally "got it right." . . .

After 17 years now, the best advice I can give is this: Focus on DESTROYING your "desire" to drink.

Most people simply try to "stop drinking" without ever addressing the false belief that drinking represents a thing of value. They never consciously attack the lie that suggests "drinking" is equal to "reward." And yet this is the root of the problem (It is the concept of "reward" that drives their desire to drink in the first place.) Tear down this false association, replace it with an accurate one (one that reflects the true nature of what drinking brings to the table—a consistent accumulated LOSS) and the rest will take care of itself.

When you get to the point where you honestly see drinking as something that can only weaken and harm you—when the "thought" of drinking alcohol becomes akin to the thought of drinking bleach or gasoline . . . when you've honestly accepted that no matter what that split second "urge" might present as a "worthy reward," the costs will ALWAYS, ALWAYS, ALWAYS end up being more than the so-called "reward" was worth; it is then the thought of drinking becomes laughably easy to ignore. . . . within just a couple years, drinking had become a non-issue in my life (which freed up a lot of time and energy for other, more productive things.) If I had known then what I know now (regarding the exact mental work that needed done) I'm sure I could have been "over it" much sooner. Simply stated, I destroyed my desire to drink (by learning to see it as the enemy of everything I hoped to achieve) and the rest is history.

Every day is progress . . . every lesson has value (especially those events we mistake for "failure.") Keep learning; keep gathering info, keep challenging the lies that drive you to harm yourself. It won't take long before progress is made. And remember, ALL progress (whether it's 1%, 5%, 10% or more) is well worth having.

I Caused Injury and Death

Ian Van Rooyen

Never thinking anything bad could happen to him, Ian Van Rooyen got behind the wheel of his car intoxicated and caused an accident that took the life of a young husband and seriously injured the man's wife. Facing prison time, he confronted his poor judgment and the pain his behavior caused. In the following speech made to high school students in Victoria, Australia, he concludes that even though he did not want to harm anyone, his decision to drive while intoxicated meant he did not care if he did.

It is with great shame and embarrassment that I relay my story to you.

One Saturday night I called a mate to see if he'd like to watch the footy [Australian rules football] over a few beers. After driving over to his place we decided to watch the game on the big screen at the pub. Again I drove. My team was winning, my mate was getting angry and the beer was tasting very good. After the game we played pool, I was winning and I was happy. At no stage did I think to monitor how much I'd drunk or how tipsy I was feeling, it just didn't occur to me. We had decided to call it a night, as I had stayed longer than I intended. On the way back we were chatting and having a laugh when we heard an almighty crash, the airbags went off, we were stunned. After checking to see if we were both ok, we both asked "what happened?" I jumped out of my car and saw another car to my left, up on the nature strip [grassy highway border]. As I got closer, my stomach sank. I could see that the car was wrapped around a pole. The pole was where the driver's door should be.

It would seem that I had hit the back of their car and caused them to lose control. Both my passenger and I didn't have a scratch on us. People were gathering around, as we were right outside some fast food stores. I ran to the other car and forced open the passenger door. I saw a young woman, blood around her nose and mouth. She was moaning, calling out for her husband. He was pushed against her, head facing me. His eyes were open—lifeless eyes—staring at me. They seemed to accuse me while I felt for a pulse. This image is what I see every morning upon waking, every night as I try to sleep and countless hours during the day. From the crash scene I was taken to the hospital, where I was looked at by doctors and arrested by police. It was then that it really sunk in. I was the one that pushed that car off the road. I, alone, am responsible for everything that has happened since.

Taking Responsibility

When I got home, I thought, what have I done? I am in so much trouble and how am I going to tell everybody what happened? Then it dawned on me, this was not about me, it is about the family of my victims, the young wife whose body and life I've shattered, their friends, my family and friends and so on.

I've read the medical reports of the injuries I've caused the young lady. They are extensive. I know that some injuries will heal, but she will never be physically 100% again. How could I ever make her feel a little bit better? The sad truth is, I know I never can. As for the man I killed, he had his whole life ahead of him, a sportsman, loved by all. All hopes, dreams and happiness gone, and for no reason.

What does it feel like to kill a man? Well, I can tell you it dominates your thoughts. It can reduce a grown man to tears at any time. Regret is a terrible thing, the relentless nightmares, just the knowledge that I have devastated so many lives keeps the pain in my heart fresh and constant. I cannot clean this stain on my soul. It's not something you can switch off, this is forever.

The Stain Is Forever

I am certain that very shortly I will be going to gaol [prison]. This, of course, scares me a lot. I've never heard anyone who's been there say that it was ok and that they wouldn't mind going back. I know that I will be sentenced for many years. I only hope this gives the families the feeling that some justice has been served. This time in prison means that any relationship with girlfriends is lost. My hopes of buying a house this year, my career and just being with the ones I love are dashed. Finding a job will be harder because I have served time in prison. This is because I thought it wouldn't happen to me.

Feeling Invincible

The usual justifications ran through my head. I'm a good driver, I can handle my alcohol better than most, and I would have to be very unlucky for anything to happen. Truthfully, I was more worried about a booze bus [vehicles operated by the police to check the blood-alcohol level of drivers] than killing someone. Of course it wasn't me who was unlucky, it was all those people I have hurt because of my stupid selfish behavior. Looking back I am amazed at my lack of responsibility. Why would I risk so much? I suppose it's because I arrogantly believed that this was something that happened to other people. I have had friends who have died in car accidents before but I could never believe that I could be the cause of one. My rationale sounds incredibly stupid when I say it out loud. If only I had tried to convince myself out loud then I would've heard how foolish I sounded. However, "What ifs" are for the future not the past.

I cringe when I hear a comment like "I'm more relaxed when I've had a few and therefore drive a bit better" or "she'll be [all] right, I'm only going around the corner" or similar things and dismissing other people's concerns. I wish I didn't ... ignore my friend's advice or ignore the truth that I knew deep inside. I can say that I would give my life if it meant I could bring back the man I killed, a man I never knew.

Going to Prison

I often look at the children I know and love and privately shed a tear at all the important things in their lives that I will miss. I do wonder what those kids will think when they ask why uncle Ian isn't there. I dread the answer more as kids believe only really bad people go to gaol. It isn't just the kids I'll miss. I think of the weddings, births, holidays away with friends and all the other special events that become fond memories in life. I'll miss those important dates, as I'll be behind bars as a result of my own stupidity.

In the first couple of weeks after the crash I was prisoner of my couch. I was so crippled with emotion that I was simply unable to move. I couldn't work, see anyone or even have coherent thoughts. Eventually I returned to work but without much enthusiasm. The constant guilt and remorse robbed me of the ability to laugh or to have a good time. When I did venture out, it was a disaster. My friends couldn't relate to what I was going through and as such I was poor company. This made me feel boring and unwanted as the downer of the group. It has taken a while but I do occasionally go out with friends but my thoughts keep me just a bit separate from them. I just don't seem to laugh anymore. Life for me goes on but it's not the same.

Another cost to this is a purely financial one. I would like you to consider how much, say, five years' salary, lawyers, court costs, massive medical expenses including air ambulance and weeks of intensive care, rehabilitation, etc., tow cars and the possibility of being sued in civil court would add up to. It sure is more than any taxi fare I've heard of. It really is enough to financially cripple someone for a long time. I know this doesn't mean much in the grand scheme of things but it is just one more thing I think about.

What Are Others Thinking?

I also wonder what do people whom I cherish, think of me? Although they've never said so, it must be terribly sad and disappointing for my parents to think of their son going to gaol. Can my friends really be proud to be associated with me? I think of all the people I've let down and this just adds to my despair. I've been told, "You just made a mistake, and you have to forgive yourself". However, I have to be honest I don't think I would easily forgive someone who killed my loved ones, if I knew it could have been avoided. I know I won't ever forgive myself as I truly feel I don't deserve [it].

Obviously I didn't mean to kill and injure people when I drove off that night, but driving when I shouldn't have means that I didn't really care if I did. This is what I find so terrible. All this death, damage and headache were totally unnecessary. I have refrained from using the term accident, as it was me who is totally to blame. This is something I cannot reconcile with my conscience. This will haunt me for the rest of my life.

CHAPTER 3

Taking Action Against
Drunk Driving

The Judicial System Can Prevent Drunk Driving Crashes

Dan Towery

After losing his daughter and her friend in a car accident that also claimed the intoxicated driver's life, Dan Towery sought to come to terms with his loss and also set out to reform the judicial system to make legal proceedings against drunk drivers more effective. In the following selection, Towery envisions law enforcement agencies working closely together to stop repeat offenders and keep the streets safer for law-abiding drivers.

On March 21, 1999, Sarah Towery and Chip Smith were killed by a drunk driver (Jeffery A. Trout) in Lafayette, Indiana. Trout was also killed. He was a repeat drunk driver offender with a long history of contempt for the judicial system. *This tragic incident need not have happened.* Since the crash we have learned a lot about how the judicial system works and about the lack of communication among various law enforcement agencies, between different states, and even between neighboring counties. Although Trout was the primary cause of the crash, there are numerous individuals, businesses, government agencies, and the judicial system, that allowed this tragedy to occur and must bear some of the responsibility.

This document outlines some drunk driving reform initiatives that will reduce future drunk driving tragedies, assign financial responsibility for irresponsible behavior, and create a more efficient judicial system. Some changes are fairly simple and should be reasonably easy to enact; others require a major shift at either the state and/or federal level to enact.

Dan Towery, "Father Recounts Tragedy," *Drunk Driving Reform Initiative*, July 25, 1999. www.ddreform.org/FatherRecounts.html. Reproduced by permission.

People Want to Ignore the Problem

People's reactions to this issue are interesting. We have found that most individuals do not want to deal with this issue, which is too scary, foreboding, or uncomfortable. Individuals do not like to think that a drunk driver may kill a loved one or even oneself in an instant. It always happens to someone else. Most people are much more comfortable with "happy" thoughts rather than thinking about their own vulnerability. This was certainly my viewpoint before that mild March afternoon.

Even those involved with alcohol-related driving issues in Indiana have tended to focus their efforts on changing the legal Blood Alcohol Level [or concentration] (BAC) from the current .10 [.10 grams of alcohol per 100 grams of blood] to .08 [.08 grams of alcohol per 100 grams of blood]. Although this is important, educating people about how many drinks it takes to reach the .08 or .10 level is more important than establishing a lower legal limit. But this discussion is meaningless when dealing with people like Trout, who had a BAC of .27, over 2 1/2 times the legal limit in Indiana and over 3 times the legal limit in states with a BAC legal limit of .08.

If stricter drunk driving penalties are enacted, some will claim that individuals' rights are being violated. But these proposed reforms are in fact in response to Sarah's and Chip's rights, which were extremely violated—they were killed and denied a future. Drunk drivers' rights are lost only because of their own actions. If individuals cannot act responsibly on their own, then it is the responsibility of government leadership to provide the rules and structure needed to protect innocent people from these irresponsible individuals. . . .

Crash Day

About a month before the fatal March 21st date, Sarah had scheduled a weekend visit to our home in Lafayette. Sarah lived just south of Springfield, Illinois, worked full-time as the office manager at an engineering firm (PSI), and was attending the University of Illinois at Springfield part-time. She was taking two classes per semester and would have graduated in May 2000 with a B.A. [bachelor of arts degree] in business and a minor in international relations. She had met Chip, who . . . worked at the same engineering firm as a drill rig operator, about six months earlier. Although we had met Chip before, this was his first trip to Lafayette. *I still feel guilty about him coming to visit us in Indiana and returning home in a box.* Sarah always seemed to have a boyfriend, but as we were scheduling the date for this visit, she asked us twice to make sure this weekend was special. She had never asked this before. We don't know how serious Sarah and Chip were, but they seemed like a couple made for each other. They supported each other, encouraged each other, and made each other happy. Chip had been a volunteer fireman for the Riverton Volunteer Fire Department since he was sixteen (his dad is chief for the Riverton Volunteer Fire department and has been a volunteer fireman for years) and was taking classes to become an emergency medical technician. The EMT [emergency medical technician] certification would allow Chip to be more competitive to become a full-time fireman.

A Special Weekend

We met them for lunch on Saturday in Lebanon, went to the IMAX [large-format] theater (Chip had not been to a 3-D movie before) in Indianapolis, and then played games and looked at picture albums (Sarah's baby pictures for Chip's benefit) Saturday night. On Sunday, I made homemade waffles. We decided to take a hike along a stream near Attica, which was also on the way home for Sarah and Chip, before we parted. Because it was on their way home, we drove separately with them following us.

About 2:45 PM we were traveling on [highway] 350 South, a city street that is straight, flat, and relatively wide (it had recently been upgraded due to Lafayette's building boom). It was a typical early spring day, slightly overcast and a little cool but pretty nice for March. This section of the road was at that time wide open with few buildings on either side. We were traveling about 45–50 MPH [miles per hour] when I noticed a pick-up truck coming toward us that had crossed the center-line. The pick-up had forced the car ahead of us over onto the shoulder, and I started to reduce speed and move to the shoulder also. After the driver of the pick-up crossed the center line, he steered the truck back to the right. As he went past us it appeared that he was using a cell phone (later it was confirmed that he was arguing with his girlfriend on the cell phone) as he was steering with only one hand. He swerved off onto the shoulder of the road, and I thought he was going into the ditch. Instead, he jerked the steering wheel hard to the left, greatly overcorrecting his trajectory and heading directly toward the Camry with Sarah and Chip.

A Terrible Crash

Margie and I saw the horrific impact in our rearview mirrors and were approximately 300 feet ahead of Chip's Camry at the time of the impact. Trout's full-size pick-up was traveling in excess of 70 MPH and Chip's vehicle was going about 45 MPH when they struck head on. Because Trout had overcorrected his steering and because of his speed, the truck's right wheels were in the air when the impact occurred. The force of the collision knocked the Camry 30 feet backwards and 30 feet to the right of the road's pavement. The Camry rolled 360 degrees. It came to rest on its wheels, pointed in the same direction it was traveling, parallel to the road. Sarah and Chip were both wearing their seat belts and the Camry's air bags deployed but the entire front of the car was pushed into the front seat. Trout's pick-up landed on its side. He was partially ejected (he was not wearing a seat belt), and the truck caught on fire. Margie and I were the first back to the scene but all we could do was tell the kids to hang on and that we loved them. They were trapped in their seats, both reclining at about a 45-degree angle and unconscious. Neither was bleeding or had any obvious injuries. *There was nothing we could do to help them.* A little later I did reach in and gently brushed glass fragments from Sarah's eyes. I was afraid the glass might cut her eyes.

A nurse in the vehicle in front of us came back to help. Sarah had a thready [clear but deficient] pulse but was not breathing; Chip had no pulse and was not breathing. A Lafayette fireman, Richard Doyle, was in the car right behind Sarah and Chip; he immediately radioed for assistance. Richard had lost his eighteen-year-old son only 1/3 of a mile further up the road in a head-on collision just four months earlier (the other driver fell asleep). A new fire station is only about a mile down the road, and the fire department personnel were at the scene very quickly. The fire in the truck was blazing more intensely with each passing minute. Four or five other motorists had stopped to help. Disregarding their own safety, they rocked the truck in an effort to get the driver out of the burning truck. After several attempts, they were able to pull him through the passenger side window.

The Scene of the Accident

After pulling Trout out and seeing his head injuries, all but one of these individuals "lost it" and left him lying just outside of the truck. The flames were now 20–30 feet in the air and the pickup was only 20 feet from the Camry. There was concern the gas tank would explode. The initial fire truck was just pulling up and I knew it would take awhile for them to get their equipment out. One of the guys who helped rock the truck and I grabbed Trout, one at each shoulder, and pulled him 20 feet away from the burning truck. Meanwhile I stood between Chip and the burning truck to try and protect him from the flames or if the gas tank should explode. However, only a minute or two passed before the fire department had their hoses out and extinguished the flames.

Richard Doyle used a stool from the Camry to break the rear passenger window and started to give Sarah CPR [cardiopulmonary resuscitation]. The paramedics could not find even a faint pulse for Chip.

It seemed an eternity before another emergency vehicle brought the "Jaws of Life" [spreading and cutting tool] which was needed to extract Sarah and Chip. We know that, for all intents and purposes, Chip and Sarah were killed instantly. The force of the impact caused massive brain injuries. Due to the seat belt and air bag, the only other injury Sarah suffered was a broken pelvis and a few scratches. (This really shows how these devices help reduce injuries.)

Because Sarah still had a slight pulse, the paramedics and fireman concentrated on extracting her from the vehicle. Both Margie and I were in shock at this time. The firemen made us stand back as they worked to free Sarah. Margie and I decided that I would ride in the ambulance with Sarah and she would take our dog home and meet us at the hospital.

Ambulance Ride and Hospital

The paramedics started working feverishly on Sarah immediately. I rode in the front seat of the ambulance. As we were pulling away, I saw two firemen placing a tarp over the Camry with Chip still in the driver's seat. I knew then that he was probably dead. The ride to St. Elizabeth hospital took about 10 minutes. During this time, they kept CPR going constantly. I was somewhat upset when Sarah threw up (something that often occurs when one receives CPR) and they didn't try to clean it up. She would have been very upset to be so messy. Upon entering the hospital emergency room ambulance bay, they cut away Sarah's bra and began to electroshock her heart into beating again. It seemed liked we stayed in the ambulance, just outside the emergency room doors, for quite some time. I lost track but they must have shocked her four or five times before her heart restarted.

I know that before the paramedics made us leave the Camry, while they were extracting Sarah, her pupils were fixed and dilated. But even when they wheeled her into the emergency room, I still thought she would recover. On the TV shows, they shock people to restart the heart all the time, and they recover. I was even thinking about the changes we would have to make at home to accommodate Sarah during her recovery.

Chip Was Declared Dead

Margie returned to the hospital, and I started to make calls to family members. We were absolutely frantic, as we only knew Chip's last name as Smith. We had no idea what his father's first name was, and when I called information, there were over 200 Smiths in the Springfield telephone directory. This anxiety was heightened, as we couldn't find out where Chip was taken. No one seemed to know anything. We couldn't understand: If he wasn't at St. E's [Elizabeth's] or at Home hospital, then where was he? We found out later that Chip was declared dead at the scene and was taken directly to the morgue. Diane Begley, the emergency room doctor on duty, informed us that she was quite concerned because Sarah was not capable of breathing on her own. Richard Doyle and his wife, Sandy, came to the hospital and sat with us till other family members began to arrive. Words cannot describe their help and comfort as we waited for more information on Sarah's condition.

The brain CAT [computerized axial tomography] scan confirmed Dr. Begley's concern; Sarah's injuries were not survivable. We wanted to know, were they 110% certain? What were the options? We wanted to keep Sarah alive until all the family members arrived and could say their good-byes. The emergency room staff felt it might be possible with drugs to keep her stabilized for just a few hours. She was moved to the intensive care unit. We also decided to proceed with organ harvest donation so Sarah's death could benefit others. All immediate family members arrived within four hours, and a more sophisticated brain scan showed there was no brain activity. The official time of death was 10:15 PM. The intensive care staff tried to keep Sarah stable, as the harvest donation team would not arrive until 6 AM. Unfortunately, the drugs needed to keep her stable were also making it impossible to harvest her major organs. We made the decision to stop the drugs and to turn off the ventilator. The machines were turned off at 12:30 AM on March 22nd.

The team was able to harvest Sarah's corneas, heart valves, and some skin tissue, because these organs are not as sensitive to the drugs as the major organs, such as the heart. Sarah enjoyed helping people and would be glad to know that even in her death she could make someone's life better. . . .

Not Another Statistic

We let Sarah struggle and make her own decisions. We knew that this was best for her, and she was very independent. But I always told her, if you ever get in a real bind, I will always be there for you, you can always count on me. *But I wasn't there for her, I couldn't help her.* I wasn't able to do anything in the two seconds it took for a drunk driver to end Sarah's and Chip's lives.

But I promised her that she and Chip would not be just another statistic, that I would do everything I could to see that their deaths prompt some type of change, that there would be fewer drunk-driving victims in the future. After all, if we can't learn from our past mistakes and initiate the needed transformation to prevent those same mistakes from occurring over and over, then what kind of society are we?. . .

Circumstances and Recommendations to Prevent Drunk Driving Deaths

1) Complete computer records and digital fingerprint analysis for tracking and fraud prevention [so authorities can revoke licenses or jail individuals who may pose a danger to others]. [Trout had prior convictions and driving while intoxicated arrests in three states under two different names.] . . .

Solution: The technology is currently available to use digitized fingerprints, take digital photos, do records checks, and have the complete file of an individual within a matter of seconds. The biggest challenge for this to be effective is that every law enforcement agency needs to be linked to a central aligned nationwide system. It is even possible that a law enforcement officer could do a fingerprint scan in the field and have the results back in seconds. The ease of using false names and fake identification to hide prior arrests and convictions would be eliminated. It is not known what the cost would be, but the advantages of such a system would be enormous.

2) Ignition interlock system or house arrest

Most states have statutes allowing ignition interlock devices for OWI [operating a vehicle while intoxicated] offenders. States have these statutes because a federal bill was passed about ten years ago, which reduced federal highway funds if the states did not allow this technology. Indiana passed such legislation and gave the judges complete discretion as to its implementation. I could only find one Indiana judge, Judge Rick Culver in Hancock County, who has been using the technology. He has used these devices consistently for five years. In fact, he has required these devices on over 1,200 vehicles and now requires these devices for every OWI offender.

The ignition interlock system looks like a CB [citizens-band] radio. The driver must blow into a straw device attached to the main unit. If the BAC is above .025, the vehicle will not start. It also has a rolling retest and many other features to make it almost full-proof. It requires maintenance every two months at which time information is downloaded from the device, including the number of times alcohol is detected while trying to start the vehicle, level of insobriety, date and time vehicle is operated, if bypass of system was attempted, and many other features. This information would be very valuable to probation officers. . . .

Solution: Make ignition interlock devices or house arrest mandatory for all OWI offenders. After six months of house arrest then the individual could have the ignition interlock device installed. The ignition interlock device would be installed on his or her car for at least two years. There should be no exceptions. This will not only reduce the number of repeat offenders but also cause the casual drinkers to consider the consequences of having too many beers and driving. The roads will be much safer. Texas just passed legislation requiring the ignition interlock for every OWI in the state.

3) Dram shop insurance [insurance for businesses selling alcohol]

Trout had 10 drinks in the space of 2 hours and 28 minutes served by Mirage bartender, James Irwin. Many of the drinks were doubles and triples, resulting in the equivalent of about 23 drinks with no food. Trout weighed about 215 lbs and the BAC of .27 works out with the expected formula. The Indiana Excise Police confiscated the surveillance video showing the number of drinks and time each drink was served. . . .

Solution: Dram shop insurance [should be] a precondition to obtaining a liquor license.

Why is there legislation requiring automobile insurance while dram shop insurance is not required in some states, like Indiana, in order to obtain a liquor license. A state statute should require a minimum of one million dollars dram shop insurance for any establishment that sells alcohol, with the actual amount based on total alcohol related sales. Perhaps then, bars would think about the potential repercussions of selling alcohol to intoxicated people. Also, if there were repeat claims against a particular bar, dram shop insurance rates would increase, perhaps making the bar owner act more responsibly.

4) *Mandatory bartender training requirement*

Numerous states require state-approved training for bartenders prior to obtaining a bartender's license. Bartenders must be able to recognize when someone has had too much to drink and to take the appropriate action to prevent them from injuring or killing themselves or someone else. While the bartender needs to screen patrons and possibly limit sales, the bar owner is interested in maximizing the number of drinks sold and increasing profits. . . .

Solution: . . . The state liquor commission shall ensure that state-approved bartender training is provided. A bartender's license shall not be issued nor employment begun until after said training has been completed. No exceptions.

5) *Habitual offender not eligible for bartender's license.*

James Irwin, Mirage bartender [who served Trout alcohol] on March 21, had the following convictions:

- OWI conviction plea-bargained to a misdemeanor

- 3/88—Failed alcohol counseling program

- 4/90—Marijuana possession; paraphernalia possession;

- 3/93—OWI; charges dropped 10/21/96 due to congested court calendar

- 1/14/93—OWI, possession of marijuana, leaving the scene of an accident, resisting law enforcement, disorderly conduct, habitual substance offender . . .

Solution: Habitual substance offenders are ineligible to obtain a server's permit and anyone on probation for alcohol or drug related convictions should be denied a server's permit.

Habitual substance offenders are unlikely to enforce laws such as not serving alcohol to an intoxicated person. While one has to make a living, there are many other choices besides being a bartender. A court-declared habitual substance offender should not be allowed to obtain a bartender's license, ever.

6) A conviction of serving alcohol to an intoxicated person causes forfeiture of server's permit.

If a licensed bartender is charged or convicted of serving alcohol to an intoxicated person, then their server's permit should be suspended upon being charged and revoked if convicted. In addition, they should not be eligible to obtain a server's permit in the future if convicted. If they weren't paying attention during their training or didn't take their responsibility seriously, then they do not deserve a second chance. Serving alcohol to an intoxicated person is like placing a loaded gun in his or her hand.

Solution: A bartender convicted of serving alcohol to an intoxicated person loses his or her server's permit and is ineligible from obtaining a permit in the future.

7) Auto insurance waivers with accountability.

Trout did not have auto insurance on his truck, with him as a listed driver. His auto insurance was cancelled in December 1998 due to the Boone County arrest for OWI in October. . . .

Solution: Accountable auto insurance waivers.

There are legitimate reasons for waivers to be used. However, there also needs to be accountability so people don't abuse the option. I look at it much like when someone cosigns a loan. One can cosign but realize that if the person defaults then you are left to repay the loan. If you sign your name for insurance coverage and there is a waiver for a particular driver, then it must be with the legal understanding that if the driver does drive, and cause bodily harm, you will be held legally responsible for restitutions.

The other option is to simply disallow any vehicle ownership or insurance coverage for anyone who has had multiple OWIs. Their vehicles are confiscated, which is what New York

State is doing for OWI arrests. They confiscate the vehicle of anyone arrested for OWI, not just found guilty.

Another option would be to have the BMV [Bureau of Motor Vehicles] require the license plates be turned in for a second OWI conviction.

8) Delaying court process . . .

Solution: Delaying court process unnecessarily results in penalty.

If the BAC is over .15 and the accused asks for a continuance and he/she is found guilty, then fines are doubled, ignition interlock time is doubled, house arrest time is doubled, and work release or jail time is doubled.

9) Probation officer caseload.

Probation officers are a very critical part of the judicial system that are often overlooked and taken for granted. . . .

Trout's probation officer indicated that his current caseload is almost 300 cases. He also indicated that to do his job well, he could probably handle about 75 cases. If Trout's probation officer had a manageable caseload would he have found out about Trout's arrest in Boone County? We will never know. Trout could then have been arrested for violating his probation.

Solution: Adequate Funding for Probation Department

In addition to giving harsher sentences, timely trials, and the like, the probation department needs the resources to oversee those on probation. Any system is only as good as its weakest link. The probation department needs the resources for effective management of cases.

10) Uniformity in charges and sentences across the country.

A person's record should travel with them regardless if they move to a different state. Many experts express dismay over the way previous OWI convictions are handled. Many times an individual can start with a clean slate just by moving to another state. States with different BAC levels are part of the problem. The way potential felonies are plea-bargained to misdemeanors makes it difficult if not impossible to know what the original charges were. Compound that with someone who moves to a different state periodically and you can end up with an individual with a number of misdemeanors when if known, the total charges and convictions would result in felony convictions and more severe penalties.

Solution: Standardize legal BAC levels, standardize felony and misdemeanor convictions, and all convictions go with individuals even if they move to a different state.

Set the national BAC of .08. Create uniform standards such as:

First OWI—ignition interlock required on all individuals or house arrest; fine plus court costs, 20—100 hours community service depending on level of intoxication, mandatory drug and alcohol counseling.

Second OWI—mandatory house arrest or ignition interlock for 3 years, 90 days home detention or 30 days in jail; 20–100 hours of community service (depending on level of intoxication); fine plus court costs; mandatory drug and alcohol counseling.

Third OWI—mandatory ignition interlock for 5 years or vehicle confiscation; 180 days home detention or 90 days in jail; 100–200 hours of community service (depending on level of intoxication); fine plus drug and alcohol counseling; weekly alcohol and drug screening.

This is an example of how it would work. Experts would develop actual sentencing. The main point would be to develop some consistency.

A Challenge to Change the Law

Kathryn Strodtman

Having lost her sister in a car crash, the author demands changes in the way drunk drivers are handled by the judicial system. She believes that repeat offenders should get help for alcoholism and be punished swiftly and more harshly to deter them from harming people again. She urges leaders to take a stand against drunk driving and asks for help in reforming the judicial system. When she wrote this section, Kathryn Stodtman was a senior nursing student.

Recently in one of the final meetings of my GEP 397 class, my teacher said that if we have not had the opportunity to stand up and challenge something during our college career, he pitied us. He pitied us for not exercising our minds to challenge the system set before us. I am a vocal student, but this time I not only want to challenge my professors, but I also want to challenge all of you who read this article.

On April 21, 2007, my little sister, Heidi, was killed by a drunken driver. I know you probably think this is just another sister on a crusade. In a way, yes, but it's not what you think.

This particular driver had a blood alcohol level of 0.235, the legal limit in Missouri is 0.08. This would be 2.94 times the legal limit. He also had just the bear minimum of automobile insurance, liability only. When he struck Heidi's car with his 2001 Dodge Ram, he was going northbound in the southbound lanes of a four lane highway. All of this happened around 8 PM. The only thing that this man could say after he killed my sister was, "Why were all of these cars in my lane?" To add insult to injury, he was not wearing a seatbelt. He

Kathryn Strodtman, "Personal Tragedy Brings New Crusade," *The Standard Online*, May 8, 2007. Reproduced by permission of the author.

lived. . . . He was taken to the hospital to be checked out and was released two days later; it was . . . a cruel irony. Heidi was not speeding and she was wearing her seatbelt. When their vehicles struck, his truck rolled over the top of her car, which crushed in the roof of her car, killing her instantly.

Why Was It Possible for Him to Drive Without a License?

Reading the police and coroner's reports is heart-wrenching. You find out so much information that hurts: One piece of information is the fact that the cooler in his truck had multiple bottles of tequila and cans of beer, some empty, some not; others being how Heidi looked in the car and what was the cause of death. Her eyes shut tight and her face constricted, bracing for the force to come. Some of the things you do not find are answers to why this was allowed to happen.

My family and I really want to know why this is only considered "involuntary manslaughter" when his blood alcohol level was 0.20. This man knowingly got into his truck and drove. He actually thought he was on a two lane highway in the country, not a major four lane highway. Obviously, this man is an alcoholic, any person who has that high of a tolerance has to be. It takes years to be able to drink that much and not suffer major complications (i.e., liver failure, death). I want to know how did he not get pulled over before? This charge comes with a sentence of five to fifteen years in the Missouri penitentiary. This man is 47 years old; my sister was 19. There is no fair deal here.

People Need to Speak Out Against Drunk Driving

So to anyone still reading, this is my challenge to you. This could be the one time you get to speak out about something that is more common than you know. I challenge you to call your state senators and representatives. Right now [in 2007] there is an emergency bill trying to be pushed through to punish people with multiple DWI [driving while intoxicated and DUI offenses with a heavier charge. This might have been his first time of being caught, but his first time was deadly. As of right now, this man is not locked up. He is back at home and more than likely driving. When this case finally comes to trial in two years (yes, it takes that long), he might be put away for 3–5 years. If this law goes through, anyone after him could be facing a lot more time in prison.

I do not mean to come across like I am vengeance-hungry. I am not that kind of person. I just do not want anyone else to try to comfort their mother who is crying inconsolably in their arms or hear their father racked with sobs so deep it scares you. I do not want anyone else to ever have to lose someone like this. Losing my only sister felt like I lost a huge part of myself. I feel terrible that our society let this man slip through the cracks and not get mandatory help for his disease.

I beg all of you to call and make known your sentiments on this. This truly can happen to anyone. Freak accidents do happen. Someone would have died that day. The car in front of Heidi had three passengers (a man, his twin brother and their elderly father) and was missed by mere inches. The car behind Heidi had a mother and daughter. If it had not been Heidi, it would have been one or all of those people in the other cars.

A Challenge to Act

If this is not a stance you want to take in college, then pick another. We have an amazing voice as students. If we stand together on any issue, we will be heard and changes made in some way. Believe it or not, student concerns do matter to a vast majority of people. If you do not like the state of things at hand, make a point of letting others know. For me, my sister is now my crusade. I hope that my crusade is successful and the law is changed, making it harder on people with multiple offenses. In this way, I hope I get to help my family heal and prevent other families from being cruelly torn apart, I hope I get to help one of you.

This man actually has no recollection at all of the accident. He still does not remember anything about the accident. Someone had to tell him, once he sobered up that he killed a person. The "remorse" he talked about during the trial never seemed real because it's hard to believe someone is remorseful when they do not remember.

His trial actually started in June, which was a very big surprise for my family and I. The first time we saw him, he smiled and stared at my mom during the entire hearing. I have never wanted to inflict pain on someone so terribly in my life. My mom cried and cried because of it, and I could not stop him from doing it.

On December 10, 2007 my family gathered for the sentencing of the man who killed my sister. We each spoke about Heidi and how the loss affected us. The judge received over 100 letters from friends, family, and teachers. Those letters turned Heidi into a real person, not just another victim. The judge said that because of all of the circumstances that he deserved the maximum sentence of fifteen years, parole after seventy-five percent is served. What hurts is that he will be sixty two when he gets out, the downward slope in life. Heidi would have been thirty four, the prime of her life.

Even though he got the maximum, I still do not feel content because you never stop crying. It is so hard to explain to someone why you cry when a certain song is played or you see a specific flower. It never gets easier, you always miss them, you just find new ways to channel your sorrow and fight to prevent it from touching anyone else.

Society Has Tolerated Drunk Driving for Too Long

Jennifer Flynn

In this emotional statement given in court, Jennifer Flynn contends that drunk driving is an act that destroys not only the lives of the people directly involved in the accident, but also those of friends and family members. Expressing her outrage at how drunk driving is treated in American society—as a slipup, not the conscious decision to put oneself and others at great risk— she recounts the devastation her family endured after Kate, her seven-year-old daughter, was killed in a drunk driving incident and pleads that the driver be punished severely.

I loathe standing before you today, knowing that I am expected to sum up the impact of the crash in a statement. It cannot be done. But I stand before you because no one should live like I do. I am here for Grace, Eamon, Colm [Jennifer Flynn's surviving children], for my family, friends and neighbors, and for the thousands of people that have been extraordinarily kind to us. It is courage that brings me here and not revenge, because it is the right thing to do.

We, as a society, have allowed drunk driving to continue. Kate [Flynn's daughter, who was killed in the collision] didn't die from cancer, cystic fibrosis or some other terrible disease which compels us to send money to a foundation, praying that scientists will find a cure. We donate all we can afford, we raise funds, we pray and we hope someone will come up with a cure. Everyone agrees that these scourges need to be eradicated.

Society Allows Drunk Driving

Drunk driving exists because we allow it to. With drunk driving, we can't just write a check and hope for the best. It requires us to look at how we have been tolerating drunk driving with insufficient jail time, inadequate charges, and ridiculous self-improvement classes. Why do we accept laws that are written in such a way that law enforcement must prove someone's state of mind? I had the blood, the confession, the witnesses, the videotape and the unrepentant sociopath driver, and people actually said to me that if he wasn't convicted of murder, at least he'll get manslaughter and some jail time.

Why would I accept that? Why do we accept that? Kate was murdered needlessly by a deliberate act. Drunk driving could be dramatically reduced tomorrow if we changed our mind-set and punished drunk drivers. It is easy to give a little jail time. It's easy to stick someone in a program. But it doesn't work. I wish I could spend Thursday nights in a class somewhere. Pay a fine. I wish I could spend 10 years in jail, buy 10 years' worth of calendars, crossing off each day until I got my life back. My tomorrow will never get better, ever. Drunk driving continues because people aren't afraid not to [drive drunk]. Punishments are not that big a deal. They are not severe enough, because society doesn't view it as the crime it should.

Drunk Driving Is Not an Accident

Which brings me to the trial. Why do we accept it when *The New York Times* writes this was a drunk-driving bungle? Bungle is the word they actually used. Bungle. Bungle is the term you should use if you drop a bag of chips or, at worst, roll through a stop sign. Kate's head was severed from her body. The entire front end [of the drunk driver's car] was embedded in Stanley Rabinowitz [the driver of the limousine in which the Flynns were riding]. To clean it up and water it down so that it is more palatable for the papers, the news, the jury and the defendant is wrong.

Setting aside how insulting that is to Kate, Mr. Rabinowitz and our families, it is a disservice to drivers everywhere to not discuss the crash as it actually happened. If it were not constantly watered down, maybe we would punish drunk driving appropriately.

Maybe if you knew that [the] crash didn't end on impact. If you knew how things unfolded after impact, people could form an informed opinion on drunk driving. Two dead, three others maimed in a "car accident," as the defense would like to paint this, doesn't even come close to describing the carnage of that night. The defendant has rights and I am a true believer in the system—but his rights do not supersede mine. And if decisions are to be made, they should be based on all the facts; and it didn't end on impact, and it should count.

Grief Is Real

Who cleans it up for me? Who cleans it up for the court officer and police officers who don't even know us and were still visibly affected during their testimony, by the horrors of July 2nd a year and a half later?. Or the EMT [emergency medical technician] and police officers that were not permitted to testify because it would be prejudicial. Who cleans us out of their nightmares? It should count for sentencing today, and people should know so that changes might be made in society's tolerance and acceptance of this crime.

I should not be dismissed as a grieving mother. What happened to me and my family should be known and should be given the weight it deserves. I sat with Kate on the Meadowbrook Parkway [the scene of the collision] and calmly and knowingly told Officer Collins, the officer stationed to sit with me, that my life was over.

There was nothing exaggerated or dramatized in that statement. Because [the driver, Martin Heidgen] drove 70 miles an hour and mowed us down with a head-on crash, I was left to pick up my most beautiful, loving, firstborn, 7-year-old daughter's head off the floor of a limousine. To sit on the ground holding her and watch helplessly those I love so much in such pain. To see my father's leg cut off and his body mangled; my husband moaning in pain and screaming for Kate, the unnatural and scary positioning of my mother, the blood and bodily remains strewn on the seats, and my helpless, scared, hurt 5-year-old daughter crying in the corner.

The Hurt Was Overwhelming

It sounds flat on paper or even stated out loud, but living it cannot be described. Driving with Kate to the hospital, crying as I knew I was getting closer and closer, knowing it was the end and kissing her goodbye. Having minutes to get it together as I was rolled into an empty corridor to wait as they opened the back entrance to the ER [emergency room] where I would meet Grace [Kate's five-year-old sister]. How scary it was to see my baby on a gurney not knowing how we would make it through the night or any day thereafter. Saying goodbye to my father as he was transferred to a hospital better equipped to treat his horrendous injuries. Letting him know how much I loved him and how peaceful Kate looked in her sleep and that she couldn't have felt any pain.

Calling [my husband] Neil's mother with the devastating news about Kate and having nothing to say about Neil's condition. How frightening it was to be at the hospital without him. How scared I was for his survival physically and mentally. Pleading into friends' answering machines to pick up the phone so that they could get to South Nassau Hospital before the state troopers I was told were sent to tell him that his daughter was dead. All the secondhand information I was getting about his condition doubting he was well enough to hear about Kate.

We watched the clock minute by minute, waiting for 7 AM so that my mother could start the first of her many surgeries, still not knowing if it was because she wasn't stable enough to be operated on or if the hospital was waiting for the surgical team. At about 7 AM, the hospital staff realized that Grace was never examined. Knowing that she was bleeding internally and would need to be watched for several days in the pediatric intensive unit.

Breaking the Bad News

Not knowing how much she knew and how much we could tell her. We spent five days in the hospital. As we were discharged, Grace and I sat in a wheelchair being rolled out to the car when she saw a newspaper with Kate's picture on the cover. I had to tell her and the boys [Flynn's sons] by myself when we got out.

We stayed with relatives for a couple of days, hoping Neil would be released and that we could go back to my mother's house together. But it would be three weeks before he was released, and we needed to get home. It was two weeks before the doctors would release my parents and my husband, transferring them to a rehabilitation facility and permitting them to go by ambulance to Kate's wake and funeral. I visited three hospitals a day, comforted my 1-year-old, 3-year-old and 5-year old, and planned a wake and funeral Mass alone. That should count, that should be weighed. "Two dead, others injured" is an unfair, incomplete depiction of that crash.

After the Mass, Neil and I went back to the rehab facility. I had just had a funeral Mass for my perfect, spectacular child, and Neil still could not come home with us. Because of his injuries, he slept in a recliner while I slept in his hospital bed, the two of us holding hands for as long as we had the strength to keep them outstretched.

Living Without a Home

Our house was being renovated by my father, and the six of us had been staying at my parents' house. Now we had no house to go home to, no one to build it, broken bodies and spirits. Friends, neighbors and strangers came together like an Amish barn-raising to build us a place where we could try our best to live. We spent four months living in one room, myself and the kids on the bed, Neil in the recliner and Kate in a small cardboard box on a shelf in the closet, next to my T-shirts.

He [Neil] spent all day crying and drinking, and all night staring at the television. For the first few months, I never spoke in the mornings, because I couldn't believe I had to live another day without her [Kate]. For the next few months, I didn't speak in the evenings, because I couldn't believe I had lived the whole day without her. My father came home four weeks after the crash and my mother 5 1/2 weeks after the crash—all of us living in one home, wailing from the pain, both mental and physical. It was helpful because we needed each other, and horrible because it is too hard to be with people you love in that much pain and not be able to help each other.

We moved back home the weekend of her birthday. On what should have been Kate's 8th birthday, we brought Kate's ashes to the beach, sprinkling her in the ocean, a place that once brought her so much joy.

Being Only Half a Person

The past year and a half required more surgeries for all of us. The physical and mental pain we live with cannot and should not be referred to and cleaned up as "also injured." I don't want to describe what my life is like, but would it make a difference if you knew how he [Heidgen] ended all of our lives because he could, because he wanted to? Would it change the way we view and punish this crime? The papers clean it up;

the trial cleaned it up. I put my makeup on and stay busy with my children, but if you knew that I was half the person I used to be, would it make a difference? It should.

I spell, count or pray to keep my mind from going to where it is difficult to come back from. The crash and living without her affects every TV show I watch, every book I read, every conversation I have, every activity I engage in, and all of the relationships I have. Food, drugs, alcohol and exercise do not provide respite. I gasp for air as I walk through the aisles of Waldbaum's [grocery store]. I get so overwhelmed with grief or gratitude when I meet the people who were so kind to us that I can't speak. I fumble over my words and am reduced to tears in seconds. I try to be the best mother, wife, daughter and friend that I can. But I am half the woman I was.

I am most happy when I am with my children, yet being with them makes me want her [Kate] more. I had four kids in six years. We didn't have a chance to grow into individuals yet. We were one unit, each a piece making up one personality. Her absence is palpable.

Growing Silent

My marriage has suffered. I have loved my husband since I was 17, but it is excruciatingly difficult to be with someone in that much pain and to feel the same way and not be able to do anything about it. I am quiet, disconnected and withdrawn. There is no conversation that follows what happened to us. There is no subject worth talking about. So I don't.

My friends and family mourn the loss of Kate and us. And we are trying. I spend time with relatives and wake up with a rash. I go to a birthday party or holiday and wake up with an infection. I sat through the trial coughing and sneezing. Living with the stress makes me physically ill. I have suffered from infections, headaches, back pain and cuts and colds that take an inordinate amount of time to heal. I can't sleep; I am incredibly sad; I wonder what we are doing here and hope Heaven is everything I want it to be.

We are good, strong people, a loving family, with close friends living in an embracing community, and every day is a struggle—a can't-get-the-door-open-to-get-air-on-my-face-fast-enough struggle. If people knew all of this, would it make a difference in the way that we punish drunk drivers? Would it force a remedy for the inadequacy of the current system? It doesn't end with "two dead, others injured"—it's not that neat. Although time will make us more resilient as we learn to live this new life, it will never be good. How we lived to get there should count for the sentencing and be known so changes can be made.

One Man Chose to End Kate's Life

Living without Kate is more difficult than I can or care to convey, but the manner in which she was stolen leaves me breathless. One man chose to end her life. The murder charge, correctly chosen because it fits the crime, was submitted under Denis Dillon, the previous DA [district attorney]. The current DA prosecuted the case.

By reporting the defense's claim that this charge was brought by [district attorney] Kathleen Rice for political motivations, without adding that it was actually her predecessor who brought the charge, is wrong. The case is not about political agendas—it is not about Kathleen Rice. It is about Katherine Marie Flynn. It is about Stanley Rabinowitz. The charge of depraved-indifference murder was chosen because it fits the crime committed.

Misleading the Public

[Heidgen's] reptilian attorneys misled the jury and the public with complaints that the charge was tantamount to intentional murder, when he was only charged with depraved-indifference murder [a charge greater than manslaughter but less than first-degree murder]. Where is the follow-up statement that challenged him on his blatant lies? How can we ever have a necessary dialogue if the public thinks we are crazy, grieving parents and that this is a political witch hunt?

If *Newsday* is going to print articles with three defense attorneys or liberal law professors who state we'll never win, where are the three retired prosecutors that counterbalance that pathetically wrong drivel. I'm not saying you have to give the victims preferential treatment, but be fair. How does it serve the public if we are just left to believe that it is a battle that can't be won?

Our crash fits the new appellate rulings perfectly. But who else will have the videotape, the number of witnesses, the sympathetic victims? Why are we writing the laws in such a way that it makes prosecuting these cases so difficult? Why do we tolerate it? And why is it not discussed in detail? We gave the media the perfect vehicle to put this dialogue out there. We all drive the same roads—the focus should be on changing the system.

No Signs of Remorse

His foul, disgusting defense attorneys have lied about how remorseful this murderer is. We know he isn't sorry because he tried to have his blood thrown out; he tried to beat the DNA [genetic] test; he allowed a defense strategy based on blatantly false distances and speeds. He showed not a scintilla of remorse throughout the entire trial. We know he isn't sorry from the letters he wrote from prison. We know from the court officers who took him to and from the courtroom. We know from the corrections officers that take him to the law library where he researches his appeal. He never grieves, he is not sad, he never mentions us. He is only concerned with himself. The remorse would not make him less guilty, but it would make him more human.

I request that he receive the maximum sentence available. He drove such an incredibly long distance the wrong way. It is the entire length of our boardwalk. To go that far and pass all of those people. To never brake or turn, when on his side of the road before the overpass are wide areas of grass on both sides. He aimed his truck right at us and plowed into us at a crushingly high speed.

He Stole Lives

He stole her life [Kate's]. He ended ours. I request that he be sentenced 25 years to life. It is not out of revenge. I take no pleasure in knowing he'll be serving that length of time. I will not be soliciting convicts to have him beaten weekly. I almost never think of him, because he is in jail and that is the way it is supposed to be. He should serve 25 years to life because it is the correct punishment for the crimes he committed. Life is worth that. Kate's life, Stanley Rabinowitz's life, and our lives.

Parent-Sponsored After-Prom Parties Keep High School Seniors Safe

Karen Chenoweth

Many high school seniors lose their lives driving home from their prom night intoxicated. The author recalls organizing a senior party to give the young adults a fun-filled evening, supervised and without the danger of being injured or killed due to alcohol use. She encourages parents to play a more active role to ensure their kids' safety. Karen Chenoweth is a former Washington Post *columnist.*

It was just before midnight, and I was already exhausted. I wasn't looking forward to staying awake all night. I was questioning why I had spent months planning a huge, all-night party for the seniors at my child's school, Albert Einstein in Kensington [Maryland]. Foolish doesn't begin to cover how I felt.

Then I started chatting with the deejay we had hired. "I love working after-proms," he told me. "My son died in a drunk driving accident nine months ago today. He would have been graduating this spring."

Oh, yeah, I thought. That's why.

Every spring, parents with children at many of the high schools in the region throw parties after proms and graduations, depending on a school's traditions. Those parties have saved lives. Although there was a terrible car accident a few weeks ago when a student fell asleep driving home from a post-prom party, it appears that this was a private party at a hotel, not a parent-sponsored event. To be on the safe side, I

Karen Chenoweth, "Saving Young Lives, One Party at a Time," *The Washington Post*, June 17, 2007. Reproduced by permission of the author.

asked the parents who signed out kids as they exited our party last month to be extra careful in gauging whether they were alert enough to drive home.

Teen Accidents Are the Norm

It seems that every year brings the same story of metal car frames entwined with prom finery, the same interviews with grief-stricken parents left with the clutter of teenage-hood but no teenager. So about 15 years ago a few creative people figured out that if a safe, alcohol- and drug-free party were provided to kids, many would go there instead of driving around from house to house drinking.

There is no foolproof way to stop tragic accidents from happening. But I firmly believe that these parent-sponsored parties can make a difference.

Of course, the parties have to be fairly spectacular to lure the kids. Each school does it differently. At my child's school, almost 100 parents spent part of the winter wrapping presents at Westfield Shoppingtown Wheaton to raise thousands of dollars for great food and decorations, the deejay, an airbrush tattoo artist, a moonbounce, laser tag, a huge blow-up obstacle course, a casino, carnival games door prizes and—my favorite—a motorized toilet-bowl race. On prom night about 85 parents decorated, prepared food, dealt blackjack, staffed the different stations and cleaned up. We had those careful sign-in and sign-out procedures as well as serious security arrangements—high schools, after all, can be volatile places.

Teens Are Grateful

But it turned out that getting into trouble was the last thing on the minds of our 400 or so partygoers. They came to relax after their prom and to have a good time, and that's what they did. Nerdy kids, theater kids, athletic kids, thug-wannabes, soon-to-be-parents, soon-to-be-college kids, soon-to-be-landscape workers, soon-to-be-retail clerks, soon-to-be-soldiers—they all came and were openly grateful for their parents' efforts to let them enjoy some final minutes of their childhood before they have to take on the responsibilities of adulthood.

As the last few of them careered around the toilet-bowl racecourse, laughing wildly and having a great time at 4:45 in the morning, I stood in awe of the energy that kids have and was thankful they were there in the school gym and not out wandering around, getting into trouble.

They have the rest of their lives for that. But for one night we kept them safe.

Victims Deserve Dignity and Compassion

Duane Bomar

Years after the author, an emergency medical technician, lost his father in a car crash caused by an intoxicated driver, he is called to the site of an accident only to find that his wife has been killed and his daughter injured by a drunk driver. Duane Bomar recounts his efforts to keep the driver in prison and to make people aware of the grave risks of driving impaired.

In 1980, the year of MADD's [Mothers Against Drunk Driving's] birth, my family moved from Sheridan, Wyoming, to a small town in Montana near my parents. My father and I were going to buy a herd of cattle and I planned to make my living as a rancher.

It was a busy summer but when my brother's baby was born in Sheridan, we all made plans to visit the newest member of the family. My wife, Marvis, and I would drive with our two children, Vicki and Jerome. My mom and dad would drive their own vehicle in order to bring back a load of our furniture.

As the kids and I loaded our trailer for the trip we heard the sirens and saw the emergency vehicles rush by. But it wasn't until later when I happened to look outside as a tow truck drove by with Dad's wrecked car that I realized something had happened to a member of my family.

A Devastating Loss

My parents had been struck by a driver so impaired [by alcohol] that the highway patrol officer suggested that had he not died in the crash, it was likely the drunk driver would have

Duane Bomar, "Twenty Years: One Family's Story," *MADDvocate*, Summer 2000. Used by permission.

died of alcohol poisoning. My father died three days later of internal injuries; my mother was injured.

My mother's injuries left her unable to walk. I carried my mother to the funeral home to make the arrangements and pick out Dad's casket. I carried her to his funeral and grave. Mom never fully recovered so I became her caregiver until her death in 1998.

Dad's death ended my dream of being a rancher so I began working in a nearby coal mine. Perhaps because of my personal experience I volunteered as part of the mine rescue team and worked as an unpaid 'third rider' with a local ambulance company. My volunteer work was fulfilling but I hoped someday to become an Emergency Medical Technician [EMT]. That dream was realized when I completed my EMT training in the spring of 1990.

Becoming an Emergency Medical Technician

My very first call as an EMT came on April 21, 1990. I was on shift with two other EMTs, Ron and Carol. The fire alarms went off first so when ours went off at the ambulance company, I assumed we would be providing stand-by at a fire. As we got into the ambulance, Carol told us we were responding to a car crash about a mile east of town.

As we crested the hill, I recognized one of the vehicles. I told Carol, 'that's my car and my family.' As we pulled up to the crash Carol told me to stay in the ambulance but I was right behind her. A sheriff's deputy tried to restrain me but my daughter had spotted me and began screaming, "Daddy!" When I reached the car where she was trapped in the front passenger seat she began screaming, "Daddy, Mom is going to die. Daddy, do something; don't let Momma die!"

Trying to Save Their Lives

My son, Jerome, had been driving and somehow escaped injury. The drunk driver had struck the passenger side of the car where my daughter was in the front and my wife in the back. The impact of the crash was so great that the rear passenger door had been ripped off and the drunk driver's car had entered my family's car. Marvis was dead. My first call as an EMT was to the crash that killed my wife and injured my daughter.

Unlike the drunk driver who killed my dad, this one survived the crash and was charged with vehicular homicide. I asked the county attorney repeatedly for information about the case to no avail. The local parole officer was new to the area but had some information.

Preparing for the Trial

I learned that the offender, Clarence Lewis, had been previously arrested for impaired driving in our county but had not been prosecuted. I learned that he'd been arrested for DUI [driving under the influence] in other states and had fled to avoid prosecution. I also learned that the offender had already pled guilty in hopes of receiving a light sentence. The parole officer told me that I had three choices if I wanted to participate in the sentencing process. He told me I could tell him my story and he would tell it to the judge; I could write a letter to the judge; or I could be sworn in as a witness at the sentencing hearing and tell my story there. I told him I would do all three.

I wrote a letter to the judge and prepared my oral victim impact statement. There was much I wanted to say to the court. Just prior to the sentencing hearing the county attorney told me that the judge had read my letter and although he had been moved by it, thought I was a 'vindictive husband' and was warning me to be careful about what I said in court. He also told me that it was likely that the offender would be sentenced to probation and that I needed to 'be prepared.'

I gave my testimony and Clarence Lewis was sentenced to 7 to 15 years in the Wyoming Penitentiary. At one point he was paroled for about a year but returned to prison because of alcohol-related parole violations. My family was not notified of his release and when I called to get more information was told that I was not a 'registered victim.' No one had ever told me that I needed to register in order to be notified of his status. In fact, no one told me about any rights I might have as a victim of crime.

I became properly registered so was notified when Lewis requested compassion parole. He was dying of cancer and wanted to die at home with his family. My family requested that parole be denied.

Clarence Lewis died in prison. I take no consolation in that but I do take consolation in knowing that I did everything I could to keep him from harming another innocent person.

It's never 'over,' but after many years of suffering and hard work, my family's pain has eased some. [My daughter] Vicki and Jerome are both married and Jerome has two children. I have also remarried and my wonderful wife and I have a beautiful daughter, Shaye Lynn Bomar, born fifteen years to the day after my dad's death.

I've shared some of my story both publicly and privately and hope that I've been able to help some other people. Based on my own experiences, I also work to insure that victims of crime in Wyoming have their own rights: to information, to participation, to some semblance of dignity and compassion. Twenty years ago and ten years ago, my family was not afforded those rights. I believe it would be different today.

Organizations to Contact

The editors have compiled the following list of organizations concerned with the issues debated in this book. The descriptions are derived from materials provided by the organizations. All have publications or information available for interested readers. The list was compiled on the date of publication of the present volume; the information provided here may change. Be aware that many organizations take several weeks or longer to respond to inquiries, so allow as much time as possible.

Al-Anon Family Group Headquarters
1600 Corporate Landing Pkwy., Virginia Beach, VA   23454
(757) 563-1600 • fax: (757) 563-1655
Web site: www.al/anon.alateen.org

Al-Anon is a fellowship of men, women, and children whose lives have been affected by an alcoholic family member or friend. Members share their experiences, strength, and hope to help each other and perhaps to aid in the recovery of the alcoholic. Al-Anon Family Group Headquarters provides information on its local chapters and on its affiliated organization, Alateen. Its publications include the monthly magazine the *Forum*, the semiannual *Al-Anon Speaks Out*, the bimonthly *Alateen Talk*, and several books, including *How Al-Anon Works, Path to Recovery Steps, Traditions, and Concepts*, and *Courage to Be Me: Living with Alcoholism*.

Alcoholics Anonymous (AA)
General Service Office, PO Box 459, Grand Central Station
New York, NY   10163
(212) 870-3400 • fax: (212) 870-3003
Web site: www.aa.org

AA is an international fellowship of people who are recovering from alcoholism. Because AA's primary goal is to help alcoholics remain sober, it does not sponsor research or engage in education about alcoholism. AA does, however, publish a catalog of literature concerning the organization as well as several pamphlets, including *Is AA for You? Young People and AA*, and *A Brief Guide to Alcoholics Anonymous*.

American Society of Addiction Medicine (ASAM)
4601 N. Park Ave, Upper Arcade, No. 101
Chevy Chase, MD   20815
(301) 656-3920 • fax: (301) 656-3815
e-mail: email@asam.org
Web site: www.asam.org

ASAM is the nation's addiction medicine specialty society dedicated to educating physicians and improving the treatment of individuals suffering from alcoholism and other additions. In addition, the organization promotes research and prevention of addiction and works for the establishment of addiction medicine as a specialty recognized by the American Board of Medical Specialties. The organization publishes the *Journal of Addiction Medicine* and the bimonthly newsletter, *ASAM News*.

Canadian Centre on Substance Abuse/Centre canadien de lutte contre l'alcoolisme et les toxicomanies (CCSA/CCLAT)
75 Albert St., Ste. 300, Ottawa, Ontario   KIP 5E7
   Canada
(800) 244-4788 • fax: (613) 235-8101
Web site: www.ccsa.ca

A Canadian clearinghouse on substance abuse, the CCSA/CCLAT disseminates information on the nature, extent, and consequences of substance abuse and supports and assists organizations involved in substance abuse treatment, prevention, and educational programming. The CCSA/CCLAT publishes several books, including *Canadian Profile: Alcohol, Tobacco, and Other Drugs*, as well as reports, policy documents, brochures, research papers, and the newsletter *Action News*.

Centre for Addiction and Mental Health/Centre de toxicomanie at de sante mentale (CAMH)
33 Russell St., Toronto, Ontario   M5S 2S1
  Canada
(416) 535-8501
Web site: www.camh.net

CAMH is a public hospital and the largest addiction facility in Canada. It also functions as a research facility, an education and training center, and a community-based organization providing health and addiction prevention services throughout Ontario, Canada. Further, CAMH is a Pan American Health Organization and World Health Organization Collaborating Centre. CAMH publishes the quarterly *CrossCurrents*, the *Journal of Addiction and Mental Health*, and offers free alcoholism prevention literature that can either be downloaded or ordered from its Web site.

Distilled Spirits Council of the United States (DISCUS)
1250 I St. NW, Ste. 900, Washington, DC   20005
(202) 628-3544
Web site: www.discus.org

DISCUS is the national trade association representing producers and marketers of distilled spirits in the United States. It seeks to ensure the responsible advertising and marketing of distilled spirits to adult consumers and to prevent such advertising and marketing from targeting individuals below the legal purchase age. DISCUS publishes fact sheets, the periodic newsletter *News Release*, and several pamphlets, including the *Drunk Driving Prevention Act*.

International Center for Alcohol Policies (ICAP)
1519 New Hampshire Ave. NW, Washington, DC   20036
(202) 986-1159 • fax: (202) 986-2080
Web site: www.icap.org

ICAP is an alcohol policy think tank sponsored by eleven major international beverage alcohol companies. ICAP publishes reports on pertinent issues such as *Safe Alcohol Consumption, The Limits of Binge Drinking, Health Warning Labels, Drinking Age Limits, What Is a "Standard Drink"?,* and *Who Are the Abstainers?*

Mothers Against Drunk Driving (MADD)
511 E. John Carpenter Fwy., No. 700, Irving, TX   75062
(800) GET-MADD • fax: (972) 869-2206
e-mail: info@madd.org
Web site: www.madd.org

MADD seeks to act as the voice of victims of drunk driving accidents by speaking on their behalf to communities, businesses, and educational groups, and by providing materials for use in medical facilities and health- and driver-education programs. MADD publishes the biannual *MADDvocate for Victims Magazine* and the newsletter *MADD in Action* as well as a variety of brochures and other materials on drunk driving.

National Council on Alcoholism and Drug Dependence (NCADD)
12 W. Twenty-first St., New York, NY   10010
(212) 206-6770 • fax: (212) 645-1690
Web site: www.ncadd.org

NCADD is a volunteer health organization that helps individuals overcome addictions, advises the federal government on drug and alcohol policies, and develops substance abuse prevention and education programs for youth. It publishes fact sheets, such as *Youth and Alcohol,* and pamphlets, such as *Who's Got the Power? You . . . or Drugs?*

National Institute on Alcoholism and Alcohol Abuse (NIAAA)
6000 Executive Blvd., Wilco Building
Bethesda, MD   20892-7003
(301) 443-3860
Web site: www.niaaa.nih.gov

NIAAA is one of the eighteen institutes that comprise the National Institutes of Health. NIAAA provides leadership in the national effort to reduce alcohol-related problems. NIAAA is an excellent source of information and publishes the quarterly bulletin, *Alcohol Alert*; a quarterly scientific journal, *Alcohol Research and Health*; and many pamphlets, brochures, and posters dealing with alcohol abuse and alcoholism. All of these publications, including NIAAA's congressional testimony, are available online.

Office for Substance Abuse Prevention (OSAP) National Clearinghouse for Alcohol and Drug Information (NCADI)
PO Box 2345, Rockville, MD 20847-2345
(800) 729-6686
Web site: www.health.org

OSAP leads U.S. government efforts to prevent alcoholism and other drug problems among Americans. Through the NCADI, OSAP provides the public with a wide variety of information on alcoholism and other addictions. Its publications include the bimonthly *Prevention Pipeline*, the fact sheet *Alcohol Alert*, monographs such as "Social Marketing/Media Advocacy" and "Advertising and Alcohol," brochures, pamphlets, videotapes, and posters. Publications in Spanish are also available.

Rational Recovery Systems (RRS)
PO Box 800, Lotus, CA 95651
(916) 621-4374 • fax: (916) 621-2667
e-mail: rsn@rational.org
Web site: www.rational.org/recovery

RRS is a national self-help organization that offers a cognitive rather than spiritual approach to recovery from alcoholism. Its philosophy holds that alcoholics can attain sobriety without depending on other people or a "higher power," which are cornerstones of Alcoholics Anonymous. Rational Recovery Systems publishes materials about the organization and its use of rational-emotive therapy.

Research Society on Alcoholism (RSA)
4314 Medical Pkwy., Ste. 12, Austin, TX   78756
(512) 454-0022 • fax: (512) 454-0812
e-mail: debbyrsa@bga.com
Web site: www.rsoa.org

The RSA provides a forum for researchers who share common interests in alcoholism. The society's purpose is to promote research on the prevention and treatment of alcoholism. It publishes the journal *Alcoholism: Clinical and Experimental Research* nine times a year as well as the book series Recent Advances in Alcoholism.

Secular Organizations for Sobriety (SOS)
PO Box 5, Buffalo, NY   14215
(716) 834-2922
Web site: www.secularsobriety.org

SOS is a network of groups dedicated to helping individuals achieve and maintain sobriety. The organization believes that alcoholics can best recover by rationally choosing to make sobriety rather than alcohol a priority. Most members of SOS reject the spiritual basis of Alcoholics Anonymous and similar self-help groups. SOS publishes the quarterly *SOS International Newsletter* and distributes the books *Unloaded: Staying Sober and Drug Free* and *How to Stay Sober: Recovery Without Religion*, written by SOS founder James Christopher.

For Further Research

Books

Anatoly Antoshechkin, *Alcohol: Poison or Medicine?* Bloomington, IN: First Books Library, 2002.

Douglas Beirness, *Best Practices for Alcohol Interlock Programs.* Ottawa, Canada: Traffic Injury Research Foundation, 2001.

Rosalyn Carson-Dewitt, ed., *Encyclopedia of Drugs, Alcohol, and Addictive Behavior.* New York: Macmillan, 2001.

Carol Colleran and Debra Erickson Jay, *Aging and Addiction: Helping Older Adults Overcome Alcohol or Medication Dependence.* Center City, MN: Hazelden Information Education, 2002.

Griffiths Edwards, *Alcohol: The World's Favorite Drug.* New York: Thomas Dunne, 2002.

Kathleen Whalen Fitzgerald, *Alcoholism: The Genetic Inheritance.* Friday Harbor, WA: Whales Tales, 2002.

Anne M. Fletcher, *Sober for Good.* Boston: Houghton Mifflin, 2001.

Gene Ford, *The Science of Healthy Drinking.* San Francisco: Wine Appreciation Guild, 2003.

Nick Heather and Tim Stockwell, *The Essential Handbook of Treatment and Prevention of Alcohol Problems.* Hoboken, NJ: Wiley, 2004.

Eric Newhouse, *Alcohol: Cradle to Grave.* Center City, MN: Hazelden Information Education, 2001.

Thomas Nordegren, *The A–Z Encyclopedia of Alcohol and Drug Abuse.* Parkland, FL: Brown Walker, 2002.

Heather Ogilvie et al., *Alternatives to Abstinence: A New Look at Alcoholism and Choices in Treatment.* Long Island City, NY: Hatherleigh, 2001.

Nancy Olson, *With a Lot of Help from Our Friends: The Politics of Alcoholism.* New York: Writers Club, 2003.

David Paciocco, *Canada's Blood Alcohol Laws: An International Perspective.* Ottawa, ON: Canada Safety Council, 2002.

J. Vincent Peterson et al., *A Nation Under the Influence: America's Addiction to Alcohol.* Boston: Allyn and Bacon, 2002.

Frederick Rotgers et al., *Responsible Drinking: A Moderation Management Approach for Problem Drinkers.* Oakland, CA: New Harbinger, 2002.

Joseph Santoro et al., *Kill the Craving: How to Control the Impulse to Use Drugs and Alcohol.* Oakland, CA: New Harbinger, 2001.

Periodicals

Mark Bellis, Karen Hughes, and Helen Lowey, "Healthy Nightclubs and Recreational Substance Use: From a Harm Minimisation to a Healthy Settings Approach," *Addictive Behaviors*, November/December 2002.

Jennifer Butters et al., "Illicit Drug Use, Alcohol Use and Problem Drinking Among Infrequent and Frequent Road Ragers," *Drug and Alcohol Dependence*, 2005.

Donald Dougherty et al., "Age at First Drink Relates to Behavioral Measures of Impulsivity: The Immediate and Delayed Memory Tasks," *Alcoholism: Clinical & Experimental Research*, March 2004.

Kristie Long Foley, et. al., "Adults' Approval and Adolescents' Alcohol Use," *Journal of Adolescent Health*, 2004.

Michael D. Greenberg, Arvind K. Jain, and Andrew R. Morral, "How Can Repeat Drunk Drivers Be Influenced to Change? Analysis of the Association between Drunk Driving and DUI Recidivists' Attitudes and Beliefs," *Journal of Studies on Alcohol*, 2004.

Paul J. Gruenewald, et al., "Drinking and Driving: Explaining Beverage-Specific Risks," *Journal of Studies on Alcohol*, 2000.

Honolulu Star Bulletin, "Aim Anti-DUI Efforts at Average People," January 16, 2006.

Iowa State Daily, "Let Two Lost Lives Change Our View of Drunk Driving," February 15, 2006.

Robert Mann et al., "Alcohol Consumption and Problems Among Road Rage Victims and Perpetrators," *Journal of Studies on Alcohol*, 2004.

Robert Mann et al., "Drinking-Driving Fatalities and Consumption of Beer, Wine and Spirits," *Drug and Alcohol Review*, 2006.

USA Today, "Our View on Highway Safety: Stall Drunk Drivers," December 28, 2006.

Andrew Woodcock, "Alcohol at Home Could Help Cut Teenage Binge Drinking," *The Scotsman* (UK), May 12, 2007.

Index